**COMPILED BY:
DR. RENEE SUNDAY, MD**

Copyright © 2025 – All rights reserved.

No part of this publication may be reproduced, distributed, or transmitted in any form or by any means, including photocopying, recording, or other electronic or mechanical methods, without the prior written permission of the publisher, except in the case of brief quotations embodied in critical reviews and certain other noncommercial uses permitted by copyright law.

Table of Contents

I. Foreword 4
Apostle Dr. Renee Sunday, M.D.

II. How to Use This Book 6
Engaging with Whole Body Blessings

III. Divine Healing Prayers 11
A collection of heartfelt prayers contributed by coauthors, organized by themes to guide readers in their spiritual journey:
- *Prayers for Faith and Trust*
- *Prayers for Physical Healing*
- *Prayers for Emotional and Spiritual Renewal*
- *Prayers for Gratitude and Praise*
- *Prayers for Specific Needs*

IV. Stay Connected 271
Join us on YouTube for prayers, reflections, and inspiring content to deepen your Christian journey. Subscribe to stay encouraged and uplifted! the QR code will be to the playlist from my youtube channel - labeled Command your day

Foreword

Prayer is the lifeline of a believer. It is not just a ritual or a duty—it is divine communication, a direct connection to the heart of God. Through prayer, we speak to our Creator, and in return, we experience His wisdom, His peace, and His boundless love. For Christians, prayer is not just part of life; it is the essence of life. It sustains us in our darkest hours, strengthens us in our weakness, and celebrates with us in our victories.

I remember one moment that forever solidified the importance of prayer in my life. As a physician, I've spent countless hours in hospital rooms, doing all I can to help people heal. One night, I stood by the bedside of a critically ill patient. The family was weary, their hope flickering like a candle about to go out. I could feel the weight of their pain and helplessness. While my medical training offered solutions for the body, my spirit knew the soul needed something more. So, I prayed.

As the prayer filled the room, something remarkable happened. The air shifted. Fear began to dissipate, replaced by a sense of peace that words cannot adequately describe. The family, once consumed by despair, joined in the prayer. While the medicine worked on their family member's body, the prayer touched everyone in the room's soul. Days later, the patient's condition began to improve, and the family shared how that moment of prayer renewed their faith and reminded them that God was still in control.

This experience, like so many others, reminds me that prayer changes everything. It doesn't just alter circumstances; it transforms us. It realigns our hearts with God's will and reassures us that He is present, even in the most difficult situations. Prayer teaches us to trust in God's sovereignty and to find strength in His promises. It is the place where heaven meets earth.

As Christians, we often find ourselves praying for healing—healing for our bodies, our hearts, our relationships, and even our communities. Healing is at the center of God's nature. He desires for us to be whole, not only in body but also in spirit and mind. This is why prayer is so crucial. It invites God's healing presence into every part of our lives.

FOREWORD

This book, Whole Body Blessings: Divine Healing Prayers, was born out of my own journey with prayer and a desire to help others experience the profound power of divine communication. Each prayer is written with the belief that God hears us, loves us, and works on our behalf. Whether you are seeking physical restoration, emotional renewal, or spiritual strength, these prayers are meant to guide you into deeper fellowship with Him.

As you read through this collection, I encourage you to approach prayer with an open heart. These prayers are not just words; they are bridges that connect you to God's love and grace. Speak them aloud, reflect on the accompanying scriptures, and allow the Holy Spirit to minister to you in ways only He can. Prayer is deeply personal, so let these words inspire your own heartfelt conversations with God.

My hope is that this book becomes a companion in your spiritual journey—a source of encouragement during trials, a reminder of God's faithfulness in victories, and a tool to help you grow closer to Him. Prayer is not just central to a Christian's life; it is the foundation of our faith and the key to unlocking God's blessings.

May this book draw you closer to the heart of God, and may your life be enriched by the healing power of His love.

In His Service,
Apostle Dr. Renee Sunday, M.D.

How to Use This Book

Prayer is one of the greatest privileges a believer has—a direct conversation with God. It's not just a one-sided act of speaking; it's a divine exchange where we pour out our hearts and, in return, receive peace, wisdom, and guidance. This book, Whole Body Blessings: Divine Healing Prayers, is designed to help you enter into that exchange. Whether you are seeking healing, strength, or simply a deeper connection with God, this collection of prayers is here to support and guide you in every season of life.

Prayer has the power to transform not just our circumstances but also our hearts. It reminds us of who we are—children of a loving God—and who He is—our faithful Healer, Redeemer, and Provider. As you use this book, my hope is that it becomes more than just a resource; I pray it becomes a companion, a lifeline, and a catalyst for spiritual growth.

YOUR JOURNEY THROUGH PRAYER

1. Start Your Day with God

Picture this: the sun is rising, and the world around you is just beginning to wake. You sit quietly with this book in hand, opening to a prayer that speaks to your soul. As you read, you invite God into your day, asking Him to guide your steps, calm your worries, and fill you with His peace. This simple act of beginning your day with prayer sets the tone for everything that follows.

Starting your day with prayer isn't just a habit—it's a declaration that God is at the center of your life. It's a moment to surrender your plans and worries to Him, trusting that His wisdom is greater than yours. Use this book as a guide to build that habit. Let the prayers align your thoughts with God's truth and prepare you for whatever the day may bring.

2. Explore Themes That Speak to You

This book is thoughtfully divided into sections, each addressing a different aspect of the Christian journey. Whether you're feeling weary, seeking healing, or overflowing with gratitude, there is a section for you. Let the structure of the book guide you to the prayers that match your current needs.

For example:

- *If you're seeking physical or emotional renewal, turn to the Healing Prayers and invite God's restorative power into your life.*

Allow the prayers of this book to meet you where you are. You don't have to go through it in order; instead, let the Holy Spirit guide you to the prayers you need in each moment.

3. Connect Prayer with Scripture

One of the most powerful aspects of prayer is its connection to God's Word. Each prayer in this book is paired with scripture to root it in biblical truth. As you read, take time to meditate on the accompanying verses. These scriptures are not just words; they are promises from God, alive and active, speaking directly into your life.

Ask yourself:

- *What is God revealing to me through this scripture?*
- *How can I apply this verse to my situation today?*
- *What does this scripture teach me about God's character and His love for me?*

Consider writing these reflections in a journal or speaking them aloud as declarations of faith. Over time, you'll find that scripture not only strengthens your prayers but also deepens your relationship with God.

4. Write Your Prayers and Reflections

Your journey through this book is deeply personal, and keeping a journal alongside it can make the experience even more meaningful. Use your journal to:

- *Record prayers that resonate with you.*
- *Write your own prayers inspired by the themes in the book.*
- *Document how God answers your prayers and how His presence shows up in your life.*

Journaling allows you to look back and see how God has been faithful, even in ways you may not have recognized at the time. It becomes a written testimony of your spiritual journey—a tangible reminder of God's goodness and grace.

5. Pray Together with Others

Prayer is powerful when shared. This book can be a tool not just for personal devotion but also for communal prayer. Use it during family devotions, church gatherings, or small group Bible studies. Read the prayers aloud, and let them guide your conversations with God as a group.

Praying together creates a bond among believers, strengthening relationships and building collective faith. It also invites God's presence into your shared space, where His peace and power can be felt in profound ways. Don't underestimate the impact of gathering in prayer—it is a reflection of the body of Christ working together in unity.

6. Make Prayer a Lifestyle

Prayer isn't meant to be confined to specific moments of need or joy; it's meant to be a constant in our lives. This book is a tool to help you build a lifestyle of prayer—one where you turn to God not only in desperation but also in gratitude, not only in uncertainty but also in celebration.

As you use this book, let it inspire you to pray without ceasing, to carry a spirit of prayer with you throughout your day. Whether you're at work, at home, or on the go, let prayer become your first response in every situation. Trust that God hears you, cares for you, and is actively working on your behalf.

7. Attributes of God and Scriptures

As you journey through this book, you'll notice that after each contributor's prayers, an attribute of God is highlighted along with a scripture. These attributes reflect God's character and faithfulness, while the scriptures offer moments of reflection and spiritual nourishment. Let these reminders inspire you to pause, meditate, and connect more deeply with the heart of God as you move through each prayer.

HOW TO USE THIS BOOK

A LIVING CONNECTION

This book is more than words on a page—it's a tool to help you experience the living, breathing connection that prayer provides. Prayer reminds us that we are not alone. It brings heaven's resources into our earthly challenges, renewing our hearts and minds. Through prayer, we align ourselves with God's will, finding peace in His promises and strength in His presence.

May this book become a source of hope, healing, and encouragement for you. Let it guide you into deeper conversations with God, strengthen your faith, and remind you daily of His unwavering love. Prayer is not just something we do—it is who we are as believers, children of a God who loves us more than we can comprehend.

Divine Healing Prayers

A Prayer of Grief

Dear Daddy-God, I come to you with a hurting and broken heart. My loved one has passed away, and I cannot seem to cope with the fact that they are no longer here.

Accepting that I cannot say hello or goodbye, share special moments, hold deep conversations, laugh, and cry with them is a challenge. Father, as your child, I need your guidance on how to navigate this pain and loss.

Isaiah 26:3 says, I will have perfect peace if I keep my mind on you, and trust you. 1 Peter 5:7 says, throw all of my cares (burden, concern, heartache, pain, challenges, etc.) on you because you care for me.

Lord, in this season of grief, I choose to place my trust in you. I am fully aware that I cannot endure this journey without you. Proverbs 3:5 - 6 reminds me to trust you with all my heart, to not rely on my own understanding, and to seek your guidance in all things.

Father, today and every day, I will intentionally seek your guidance and direction; trust you with my heart and mind; and know you will always be there to care for me.

In Jesus' name. Amen.

Renew My Mind

Gracious Heavenly Father, I have come to a place in my life where it is imperative to renew my mind. I am constantly bombarded and surrounded by wickedness and evil, wrapped up as good and truth.

Your word says, "And be not conformed to this world: but be ye transformed by the renewing of your mind, that ye may prove what is that good and perfect, will of God".

Lord, I need to trade the negative thoughts and images for your Word and truth so I can be transformed into the disciple you have called me to be. Help me renew my mind to overcome limiting beliefs and worldly ideologies contrary to your Word.

Lord, I want my mind to be renewed so I can live according to your will and not be afraid to stand on your principles. Living according to your will means that I need to pray (have a conversation with you), read, study, and meditate on your Word (search the scriptures for clarity and let them marinate in your mind and spirit), and sometimes sacrifice pleasures, drown out the world, and turn my heart towards you.

In Jesus' name.

God's Will

Heavenly Father, I know that your will is best for me. Jeremiah 29:11 speaks of plans you have for me. I pray that my will aligns with your Word. Teach me your ways as I surrender my life to you.

Your Word says, If I seek Your Kingdom (will) first, and Your righteousness (way), you will provide me with what I need, Matthew 6:33. You also said, "Rejoice always, pray without ceasing, give thanks in all circumstances, for this is the will of God in Christ Jesus for you," 1 Thessalonians 5:16-17. In addition, 1 John 5:14 tells me, I can ask anything according to your will and you will hear me.

Lord, remove the scales from my eyes, heart, mind, and soul so that I may clearly see, hear, and understand your will for my life. According to your Word, I must have a solid relationship with you to know, love, and trust you. I must spend time with you to learn and obey your voice for guidance and direction.

Help me to seek your will so that I will not forsake you and intentionally thwart the plan (your will) that you have designed for me.

In Jesus' Name

Help In Trouble

Father God, I am in trouble and seemingly have nowhere to turn or have a safe place to hide. My enemies are trying to destroy me because of my defiance of their laws and my love, faith, and obedience to you Word.

As I cry out to you, please hear me. In Psalms 91, your Word says, if I dwell in your secret place, you will hide me. You are my safe place and defense; I can trust you to deliver me from the enemy.

Although many evil and terrible things that happen during the night, you will not let what is being done come near me. Your angels will be given authority to watch over me, keep, and hold me up, and not allow me to be injured.

In addition to the protection, 1 Peter 5:17 tells me to cast all of my burdens (anxiety, emotions, fear, discouragement, disappointment, etc.) on you and you will keep me.

Lord, please help me to give you my trouble and everything that will hold me back from serving you. Let me recall Isaiah 54:17, decree, and declare, "No weapon formed against me shall prosper".

In Jesus' name

Praise Always

Father, Psalms 34:1, Lets me know I should choose to bless you at all times and to let your praises flow from my mouth. I will not mute my praise; the humble will hear it and be glad (have hope).

It is not always easy to have hope or keep praises on my lips, but I choose to believe your Word. When I choose the door of praise, perhaps the present trial or challenge may not seem so bad.

Lord, help me recognize the triggers that will cause me to grumble and complain instead of praise you. Praise is not an option but a command. You have done so many wonderful things in my life and for me. When I think of how AMAZING you are and how I am fearfully and wonderfully made, I have to take some time every day and praise you.

Sometimes life causes me to waste time pondering negative things and situations. However, when I think of your goodness, mercy, and grace, I cannot help but praise you.

Lord, help me keep a perpetual praise in my mouth because you are in control and my trust is in you.

In Jesus' name

WRITTEN BY:

Evelyn D. Lynch

VICE PRESIDENT AT C. L. LYNCH MORTUARY INC.

Evelyn D. Smith-Lynch is Vice President of C. L. Lynch Mortuary Inc., where she fosters customer and business relationships, curates educational workshops, and leads community outreach initiatives. With over 35 years of experience in customer service, she is recognized for her leadership and organizational expertise.

Evelyn holds dual Bachelor's Degrees in Business Administration and Management, a Master's in Organizational Leadership, and a Certificate in Biblical Studies. Before joining C. L. Lynch Mortuary, she spent 32 years at the Los Angeles Department of Water and Power (LADWP), where she notably developed the first supervisory training program and led a major customer remediation project.

A passionate mentor and coach, Evelyn has served in leadership roles with LADWP's National Society of Black Engineers, Society of Women Engineers, and Toastmasters. She also holds board positions in the Alma Smith Scholarship Fund and the Affinity Group.

In ministry, Evelyn has been Director of Christian Education for over 25 years and facilitates marriage classes with her husband, Elder Courtney Lynch. She is a speaker, workshop leader, and author of several works, including I'm A Survivor – My COVID Journey and Girls Like Me Thrive Workbook and Journal.

Evelyn's unwavering faith, her 30-year marriage, and her love for helping others inspire her to empower people to live their best lives. Connect with her at www.evelyndlynch.com or via email at info@evelyndlynch.com.

 www.evelyndlynch.com

God is Faithful

"THE LORD IS MERCIFUL AND GRACIOUS,
SLOW TO ANGER AND ABOUNDING IN
STEADFAST LOVE."
(PSALM 103:8)

My Doubt. God's Grace. Seeking Clarity When Life Is Not Okay

Dear Heavenly Father,

We come before You with hearts that sometimes feel heavy, weighed down by life's burdens and uncertainties. Lord, You know that there are days—sometimes even seasons—when things are simply not okay. In those moments, we are grateful that You invite us to come, to sit with You, and to pour out our hearts. Just as You promised in Isaiah 1:18, You call us to reason together with You, to bring our confusion, our fears, and our hopes into Your presence.

Father, we pray that You help us walk through our thoughts, feelings, and emotions, whether they are right, wrong, or indifferent. Help us surrender them all to You. We ask that You bring clarity where there is confusion, comfort where there is pain, and joy where there is sorrow. Settle the matters of our hearts, Lord, and in doing so, fill us with Your peace that surpasses all understanding.

Restore our hope and reignite our joy, Father. Remind us that in You, nothing is too broken to be healed, and no situation is beyond Your power to redeem. We trust You with our hearts and our lives. In Jesus' name, we pray. Amen.

A Prayer for Renewed Hope and Unshakable Joy

Heavenly Father,

Today, we come before You, weary from life's trials yet longing to feel the warmth of Your presence. Lord, You are our refuge, our strength, and the wellspring of all joy. Even when life feels uncertain and our hearts are heavy, we choose to turn to You, trusting in Your promises and Your perfect love.

Father, we ask that You breathe new life into the weary places of our souls. Restore to us the joy of our salvation and awaken a hope that cannot be shaken. Remind us that You are a God who redeems, who restores, and who makes all things new in Your time.

Teach us to see beyond today's struggles and lift our eyes to Your eternal promises. May Your peace, which surpasses all understanding, guard our hearts and minds as we walk boldly in faith.

Lord, let Your light shine through us as a beacon of hope to others. May our renewed joy be a testimony of Your grace and power. Thank You for being a God who never fails and who carries us through every storm.

In Jesus' mighty and beautiful name, we pray. Amen.

A Prayer to Embrace God's Joy and Strength

Loving Father,

Thank You for this beautiful day and for the gift of life. No matter what challenges we face, we know that You are the source of our strength and the lifter of our heads. You remind us, Lord, that even in the darkest valleys, Your joy is our strength, and Your love is the firm foundation on which we stand.

Today, we choose to cast aside fear, worry, and doubt. Instead, we step boldly into Your presence, knowing You have good plans for us—plans to prosper and not harm, plans to give us a hope and a future. Lord, fill our hearts with gratitude and our spirits with unshakable joy. Let us laugh again, hope again, and dream again, knowing You are working all things for our good.

Help us to shine Your light wherever we go, spreading kindness, love, and encouragement to those around us. May we be a reflection of Your peace and joy, inspiring others to trust in You.

Thank You, Lord, for never leaving us, for carrying us through life's storms, and for filling our hearts with hope anew. We praise You for who You are—faithful, loving, and true.

In Jesus' name, Amen.

A Prayer for Courage and New Beginnings

Gracious Father,

We stand before You today with hearts open to Your guidance and hands lifted in surrender. You are the God of new beginnings, the One who turns ashes into beauty and mourning into dancing. Lord, we thank You for the fresh opportunities You place before us, even when we feel unprepared or uncertain.

Father, we ask for courage to step into the unknown with confidence, knowing that You go before us and prepare the way. Remind us that You have not given us a spirit of fear, but of power, love, and a sound mind. Let us walk boldly, trusting that Your plans for us are good and full of purpose.

When we face obstacles, remind us that Your strength is made perfect in our weakness. When doubt creeps in, let Your promises flood our minds with peace. Give us wisdom to discern the steps we need to take and faith to move forward, even when we can't see the whole path.

Thank You, Lord, for being the author of our stories and the rock we can stand on. We trust You with every chapter and give You all the glory for what is yet to come.

In Jesus' name, Amen.

A Prayer for Trusting God's Plan

Faithful Father,

We come to You today with hearts longing for guidance and assurance. In a world full of uncertainty, it's easy to hold tightly to our own plans and ideas, yet You remind us that Your ways are higher and Your plans are always good.

Lord, teach us to trust You fully. Even when the path ahead seems unclear, help us to remember that You are the God who sees the end from the beginning. Strengthen our faith to believe that every step we take is part of the masterpiece You are weaving in our lives.

When fear and doubt try to take root, remind us of Your unfailing promises. Fill our hearts with confidence that You are working behind the scenes, orchestrating blessings beyond what we can imagine. Let us rest in the truth that Your timing is perfect and Your plans are for our ultimate good.

Father, we surrender control to You, knowing that You are a loving and faithful God. We trust that You are leading us toward a future filled with hope and purpose. May we walk forward in peace, guided by Your wisdom and held in Your unchanging love.

In Jesus' name, Amen.

WRITTEN BY:

Rebecca Tolleson

AUTHOR, WIFE AND MOTHER

I am a wife of 26 years, a mother to 2 (23yrs and 18yrs). I have stumbled around my purpose most of my life but with focused prayer finally began to realize the path God has for me. I published my first book in 2024, "Overcoming Emotional Barriers: Strategies for Women to Break Free and Thrive", and published a companion journal shortly after.

I am also working on a devotional book and prayer journal to publish soon. I am going thru training to start my own color boutique that will help women find their best look and feel confident in their own skin while seeing their true worth.

- @TollesonCreative & @BeckyTolleson
- @tollesoncreative and @rebeccatolleson
- admin@tollesoncreative.org

God is Our Healer

"HE HEALS THE BROKENHEARTED AND BINDS
UP THEIR WOUNDS."
(PSALM 147:3)

Holistic Prayer for Healing, Peace & Truth

Based on Jeremiah 33:6

"הִנְנִי מַעֲלֶה לָּה אֲרֻכָה וּמַרְפֵּא, וּרְפָאתִים וְגִלֵּיתִי לָהֶם עֲתֶרֶת שָׁלוֹם וֶאֱמֶת"

"Behold, I will bring her health & healing, I will heal them and reveal to them abundant peace and truth."

Lord God Almighty, Eternal One,
El Shaddai, Your will be done.
Great Physician, bring Your light,
Heal the broken, restore our sight.

Pour Your peace where pain resides,
In Your truth, let health abide.
Breathe new life into each soul,
Make the wounded body whole.

Abba, Father, calm our fears,
Dry our ever-flowing tears.
Send Your wisdom, pure and true,
As we lean in close to You.

From Your throne, let healing flow,
Through every heart, in every woe.
Mend what's lost, repair with grace,
In every corner, fill the space.

For in Your hands, true peace we find,
And strength for body, soul, and mind.
With faith, we trust Your power divine,
Great Physician, our lives align.

El Shaddai, we seek Your care,
Your truth and peace beyond compare.
With every breath, with every day,
Lord, heal us in Your perfect way.

You are the One who makes us whole,
Your love, O Lord, restores the soul.

Amen.

Finding Hope: A Wife's Journey of Forgiveness and Healing in Marriage

O God, my healer, hear my plea,
You've walked this painful road with me.
In betrayal's shadow, my spirit cried,
Yet for my children's sake, I stayed inside.

"With lovingkindness, I've drawn you near,"
 I held to these words, though pain was clear.
Despite the hurt, my heart held on,
Hoping he'd turn back and be reborn.

The weight of loss, of trust betrayed,
In silent nights, alone I prayed.
Yet I clung to ahavah, Your boundless love,
To guide my heart like a gentle dove.

"Though the mountains fall, and hills remove,"
Your mercy, O Lord, remains to soothe (Isaiah 54:10).
You bound up my wounds, gave me peace anew,
Until love was reborn, fresh as morning dew.

Today, I thank You, Almighty One,
For healing our hearts, for what You've done.
My husband now stands as the man of my dreams,
In a marriage restored by Your loving streams.

Forgiving Betrayal: A Husband's Journey to Healing and Renewed Love

O God, my refuge, hear my cry,
In the wake of her betrayal, I wonder why.
I chose forgiveness, though it broke me deep,
For our children's sake, and the vows we keep.

You love unfaithful Israel with patient grace,
Choosing ahavah — a love that will not erase.
Though trust was shattered, I turned to You,
Asking strength to rebuild and start anew.

"For I have loved you with an everlasting love,"
Your words sustained when strength grew rough.
Like Hosea, who called his wife back home,
I chose to forgive, though she had roamed.

It wasn't weakness, but faith's strong hand,
That kept me steady, helped me stand.
The path was hard, yet in time I see,
A marriage reborn, stronger than we dreamed it could be.

Today, I thank You, God above,
For showing me the depths of love.
For our children's peace, and the bond we've renewed,
Our hearts are restored, our foundation made true.

Healing and Forgiveness of Parental Abuse: Breaking the Cycle of Generational Pain

Almighty, healer of wounds unseen,
Guide my heart through what has been.
My parent's pain became my own,
In shadows of hurt I once had known.

But I choose to forgive and let love in,
Understanding the struggles they held within.
For they faced trials I may never know,
And still, some seeds of goodness did show.

You teach, "Honor your father and mother," to me,
So I find what was good, as I set my heart free.
I see resilience, strength to endure,
Through pain they faced, they found no cure.

Yet I choose today a gentler way,
To heal the past, come what may.
May their memory guide me to grow,
In love and kindness I choose to sow.

Thank You, O God, for strength anew,
For helping me forgive and follow through.
I honor them now by breaking the chain,
Offering others love, not pain.

Prayer for a Lost Child's Return to Faith and Healing

O God of mercy, hear my plea,
My daughter's lost, so far from me.
In shadows deep, she's gone astray,
I failed to guide her in Your way.

She wandered down to sin's dark road,
Burdened heavy by a hidden load.
I could not shield her from pain and lies,
And now I see with tear-filled eyes.

"Train up a child in the way she should go,"
Yet I faltered, and she did not know.
I cry for her lost, forsaken years,
I bring You now my heart, my fears.

Almighty One, draw her near,
In Your light, erase her fear.
Restore her heart and let her see,
The path back home, the road to Thee.

Thank You, O God, for hearing my prayer,
For leading her back with tender care.
She's found her faith, her path anew,
To raise her children strong and true.

Now, like a tree by the water's side,
She'll walk in Your ways, Your word as
her guide.
For Your mercy endures, forever to stay,
Guiding us both on Your holy way.

WRITTEN BY:

Mayim Vega
NATUROPATHIC HERBALIST & HOLISTIC LIFE COACH

Mayim Vega is a former NASA Computer Scientist turned holistic healer after facing a personal health crisis, which the modern medical system could not solve. In 2009 she founded Arukah.com, which offers a Holistic Healer Certification program, focusing on the three pillars of Naturopathic Herbalism, Holistic Life

Coaching, and Online Business & Marketing to empower people to achieve maximum impact in the world as holistic healers.

Mayim combines her scientific background, natural healing methods, and faith in Creator & Great Physician to guide others on a path to personal and professional well-being.

 www.arukah.com

God is Our Strength

"THE LORD IS MY STRENGTH AND MY SHIELD;
MY HEART TRUSTS IN HIM, AND HE HELPS
ME."
(PSALM 28:7)

God's Four Legged Gifts

Thank you Heavenly Father for loving us so much that you bestowed upon us your beloved animal kingdom to serve & guide us in the ways of Spirit. Help us to recognize this sacred kinship & to work ceaselessly to heal this beautiful broken tapesty.

Both our precious pets & the wild magesty of the natural kingdom are your great gifts to us and offer us the path to unconditional love - let us learn from them to weave this into our tangled lives. Show us through their compassion & loyalty that we can live unwaveringly , safe in the knowledge that we can both give & receive these gifts ---

Thank you for allowing your beloved creatures in all manner to be WayShowers in our life journeys & to guide us to become the best versions of ourselves.

Finally, thank you for perhaps the greatest gift of all - the eternal enduring love for us that not even Death can deny, break or abandon, unlike humans.

And the gratitude & joy of knowing they are as close as a heartbeat, a thought or even a tear away...

Angel Paws

God, I remember you telling me, during a really bad time a couple of years ago - I was feeling so alone and having trouble feeling my connection to you - you said "Look for me in the paws" - there you will feel my love and regain your connection to me."

And I cried, grateful for any chance to be able to feel you again and such humbleness of spirit and find that yet again my beloved pets were going to save me...

I began to see where you would give me angels with Paws to guide me through the shadows and traumas of my childhood ever by my side, drying my tears with their reassuring kisses, unspoken promises to stay with me and heal my heart. These, my best teachers giving me the deepest truths, the lessons I most required, but couldn't learn from my human family and friends.

Your love for me and support flowed through these 4-legged Angels day and night, giving me the courage to trust the that truth coming through, my connection to you. I knew finally that you had never left, would never leave me no matter what...

Teaching Paws

Thank you Father for showing me the lessons of my life through my animals - when I could hear no one else, When I so deeply needed to feel your love -there were paws and wet noses, sloppy kisses, head butts and hugs to transmit your message to me - reconnect the circuits, creating laughter when there had been fear, pushing courage forth from hesitation.

Both tiny and thunderous, they gave me my first lessons in loyalty, staying in the face of harshest punishment, licking away, escaping tears, Forever by my side...

Knowing that I had night terrors, they kept watch lulling me to sleep wrapped in their soft, sweet, fur...When mistrust entered and tangled my world, their guidance reigned supreme... They watched my heart learn, grow and break and always offered soft paws ready to heal - Grey muzzles and kind eyes taught me the value of time and not rushing to decisions - to value myself - Always just as I am - They taught me that I didn't have to earn their love ever...

What my friends learned in church, you gave me through my angel animals - Throughout my life you have allowed them to be my confidants, my teachers, my healers my direct line to you until I was strong enough, clear and healed enough to connect on my own - I am so grateful for my Angel Paws...

The Final Goodbye

Here we are yet again, Lord. I Surrender, my beloved pet unto you to make whole and healed... I've known for a while now that he had received the call to return home. Yet the strength of our bond tied him so to me, to my heart that neither of us was ready yet for this final goodbye...

I tried so many times to tell him I'd be okay, yet my glistening eyes. belied my words. I went to you in council each time, asking for just a bit longer, a few more moments to hold him close to my heart, finding more memories to share for his journey...

You blessed my life with his presence and filled the chasm in my heart created by humans. He became my WayShower through the shadows and pain, leading me with love and your own light... My very own Angel wrapped in the softness of fur...

Please Lord, help me put aside my own pain and honor his life of love and service by accompanying him with all my love for him every step of the way, recognizing the sacred gift of this journey...

Let me wrap him with my love and my heart let courage and strength replace the fear and the pain and help me to remember all the truths that he has taught me... And that this is just a new beginning for us... He is never further than my heart...

Moonlight Walks With God

As I walk out into the deep dark quiet of the night, the moon casts her cool reflection softly down upon me And I know I am not alone for I feel your love and her stillness and perfect presence.

What cares may have befallen me during the daylight hours melt within the moon's radiant... majesty and I know that you have sent her to comfort me

It has always been this way between us since my cradle days. The night was meant to be only my silent time to commune with you, and only you

As the world sleeps my heart lies awake, my soul speaks up - Catching river tears falling softly... Pouring out my questions to you ...You send rainbow answers and healing moonlight

I find it hard to feel alone with you during the day... Too much of the world stands firmly in my way... I search for you, calling out...So much noise chaos... My heart dreams of the night

Moonless nights too have their very Beauty...You breed the love down and it fills my jagged edges softening where I'm frayed shoring me up wholly

Sustaining my spirit hat I may continue into the day again...Though you are everywhere always for everyone - Our nightly walks keep me in faith...

WRITTEN BY:

Dr. Tricia Working

AMAZON INTERNATIONAL BEST SELLING AUTHOR & WORLD-RENOWNED ANIMAL MYSTIC, HEALER, AUTHOR, SPEAKER, AND ORDAINED MINISTER

Dr. Tricia Working is an Amazon International Best selling author and world-renowned animal mystic, healer, author, speaker, and Ordained Minister, facilitating conscious connections with the animal kingdom as a certified spiritual coach counselor. She leads transformative conversations on how animals serve as guardians of consciousness, calling in a higher awareness and commitment not just to animals, but to humanity.

Tricia believes that spiritual growth, mindset, and paradigm shifts can occur through connection to animals; even our household pets are here to provide guidance. She shares how to incorporate these transformative experiences in her groundbreaking book series, The FurAgreements, and her wildly conscious conversations through The Epiphany Series.

Southern, Sassy, and a special kind of spiritual, Dr. Tricia is indeed a cat of many magical colors. She is known globally for her unique understanding of the final moments in life and her loving ability to assist pets and their families with ease and grace as they journey through the final goodbye transition process.

She stands by her promise that once you read her book, you will never see animals in the same way. Dr. Tricia is an Atlanta, Georgia native with seven years of experience in shelter management; she founded Paws for Thought Animal Foundation in 1993 and now lives in the Southern United States with her abundance of furry friends.

You can connect with Dr. Tricia at DrTriciaWorking.com.

 DrTriciaWorking.com

God is Our Restorer

"I WILL RESTORE TO YOU THE YEARS THAT
THE SWARMING LOCUST HAS EATEN."
(JOEL 2:25)

Jehovah - Rapha our Healer

Heavenly Father, Almighty God , Our Creator, You are the Lord who heals. We cry out to you for divine healing for those who need a spiritual healing, in healing in their mind, a healing in their physical body, a healing from the inside out .

Lord God You are Jehovah Rapha - be glorified . We trust You Lord Your word declares in Jeremiah 30:17 "I will restore your health and heal your wounds. We stand in faith we believe You Lord. We trust You will watch over your word to perform it"

We thank You in advance for Your mighty acts . We love and Honor You for who you are in Jesus Holy Name Amen. 🙏

A Pure Heart

Lord God, we thank you for being who you are. You created us in your image and likeness. You are love our desire is to be like You to have a pure heart, to love our neighbor as ourselves.

Lord help us to guard our heart with all diligence for from it comes the issues of life. Lord you heal the broken hearted and Yoi bind up their wounds. Lord let our heart reflect good motives and intentions. Father cleanse our heart , Lord our heart is for You.

In Jesus precious and Holy Name Amen.

Fearfully and Wonderfully Made

Lord God, we honor You, we exalt You, we adore You. Oh Lord You are great, there is none like You. Who is man that You are mindful of us. Before we were conceived in our Mothers womb, You knew us.

We were shaped in iniquity and conceived in sin, yet You declared that we were fearfully and wonderfully made. Lord heal us from the inside out that we would be whole and complete in You. Heal the scars and wounds from the experiences of trauma, abuse, words that were intended to harm .

The scars may remain but the healing by the touch of Your hand Your words that penetrate beyond the surface of the pain. Jehovah Rapha do what only you can do. Restore the wholeness of our being fill us with Your Love Your Joy and Your Peace. We are grateful. Just one touch from the Master .

In Jesus Name Amen.

As A Man Thinketh so is He

Sovereign God, Sovereign King, You are Almighty God. Lord we surrender our all to you. Let our will align with Your Will. Lord You are all wise, all knowing, You see everything, You hear everything, You are always with us. Lord let this mind that be in Christ be also in us.

Lord clear the minds of those who are living with a mental illness. Lord we believe Your word we cast down every imagination that exalts itself above the knowledge of Christ. Lord mental illness has to bow to you at the name of Jesus every Knee will bow every tongue will confess that You are God. Lord Heal deliver and set the captive free. Lord God there is nothing too hard for you. All things are possible with God to those who believe.

Lord we stand in the gap for those who cannot believe for themselves. Lord we ask Lord that you cover the minds with the blood of Jesus we believe the blood works, the blood washes, the blood cleanses, the blood of Jesus has miraculous power. Lord you sent your word and it heals, it will not return to you void, it will accomplish that which you send it fourth to accomplish. Lord bring those affected by mental illness to themselves - restore their minds. You oh Lord are our Healer, You oh Lord are well able to do exceedingly, abundantly above all we ask or think according to the power at work within us.

Thank You Lord in advance on behalf of all who struggle with issues of the mind in our families, in our church family, in our community, and in the work place. Lord do what only you can do we trust you we believe you in Jesus name amen.

Relationships are Important

Lord God, Heavenly Father, Our Creator, Abba Father, Wonderful Counselor, Prince of Peace, Jesus the center of our joy, Immanuel God is with us. Lord our desire is to strengthen our relationship with you, in our prayer time, our worship and in our daily walk.

Lord do not allow us to become overly confident, in having an apperance of godliness that we neglect the sweet fellowship of being in your presence. Lord we know that You have began a good work in us and you will continue to perfect us until the day of Christ Jesus. Lord we want to please You. Lord Your word says that if a mans ways are pleasing to God even his enemies are at peace with him. Your word declares as much as possible we are to make every effort to be at peace with all men. Lord its not always easy but we do know it is possible because it is your expectation for us. Let us agree with our adversaries quickly. Lord let us forgive others as you have forgiven us. Let us cling to your word and taste it to see that the Lord is good. Lord we need you in platonic relationships, marital relationships, relationships with our children, relationships with our brothers and sisters in Christ. professional relationships.

Lord we thank you for the gift of the Holy Spirit, Help us Lord to be sensitive to the promptings of the Holy Spirit, increase our discernment and help us to walk in love. Lord let us be empathetic towards others, Your word declares if You be lifted up , Your will draw all men unto You. Lord we pray that our interactions with others will point them toward You. Let others see the Christ in us. Let your light shine through us that others will see our good works and glorify you our father in heaven. This we ask in the name of Jesus Amen.

WRITTEN BY:

Ramona Gray

EDUCATOR AND MINISTER

Above all else, I am a daughter of the King (JESUS).

I am a native of New Orleans, Louisiana I currently reside in Fort Worth, Texas, United States Navy 20 years honorable discharge Texas Juvenile Justice., Educator Special Education,

Retired BS History Political Science MS Psychology M.Ed emphasis in Literacy Currently working to compete dissertation Doctorate in Biblical Counseling.

I am a Minister in my local church The Chosen Vessel Cathedral Bishop M.L. Sapp Senior Pastor I have 2 adult sons they also reside in Texas the oldest in Austin, My younger son in Houston Texas . I have a beautiful Grand daughter- Brooklyn who is a freshman this year in High School.

(f) Ramona Gray

(○) @Mona_gray

God is Worthy of Praise

"LET EVERYTHING THAT HAS BREATH PRAISE
THE LORD! PRAISE THE LORD!"
(PSALM 150:6)

A Mother's Prayer Letter For Her Daughter

Dear Daughter my prayer for you is that you continue to move forward in Christ and continue to make Him your number one priority as you pursue all the blessings He has in store for you.

I decree and declare that the favor of the Lord will continue to surround and encompass you as with a shield in every area of your life. Always remember to allow the Lord to order and ordain your steps so that you can be kept rooted and grounded in the center of His perfect and divine will.

I believe that the Lord has anointed and appointed you to step into your calling for such a time as this. Just remember to stand on the foundation and principles of Jesus in everything you do. Remember that it is God who gives you the power to obtain wealth, not the world.

I count it an honor and a privilege that God chose me to be your Mother. I pray that God blesses you with a man after His own heart to be a loving husband to you. I also pray that God will bless you with a sweet daughter just like you so that maybe one day pray this same prayer for her.

In Jesus' Name.

A Prayer for Our Pastors

Heavenly Father,

I thank You for the gift of pastors, those You have called to shepherd Your people and proclaim Your Word. Today, I lift up every pastor to Your throne of grace, asking for Your divine strength, wisdom, and anointing upon their lives and ministries.

Lord, equip them with everything they need to fulfill the calling You've placed on their hearts. Fill them daily with the power of the Holy Spirit, guiding them in truth and righteousness as they lead and serve. Give them boldness to preach Your Word with clarity and conviction, standing firm in the face of challenges.

I pray for their personal lives, Lord, that You would bless them with rest, health and peace. Surround them with support, encouragement and godly friendships. Strengthen their families and protect them from any attacks of the enemy.

Grant our pastors wisdom in decision-making, compassion in counseling and joy in their service. Renew their spirits when they feel weary and remind them that their labor in the Lord is never in vain. May they continually abide in Your presence and be instruments of Your glory.

In Jesus' Name, I pray. Amen.

A Prayer for Our Government

Heavenly Father,

I come before You today to lift up our government and its leaders to Your throne of grace. Your Word declares that all authority is established by You, so I ask for Your guidance, wisdom and divine intervention in every decision made on behalf of the people.

Bless our leaders with integrity, humility and a heart that seeks righteousness. May they govern with justice and fairness, always prioritizing the needs of the people they serve over personal agendas. Surround them with godly counselors and advisors who will encourage them to pursue what is right and pleasing in Your sight.

Father, I ask for unity among those in authority. Remove division, strife and selfish ambition, replacing them with collaboration and a shared vision for peace and prosperity. Protect our nation from corruption and any plans of the enemy that seek to bring harm or discord.

I also pray for our citizens, that we would uphold one another in love and respect, honoring those in leadership while holding them accountable in truth. May Your will be done in our government, and may this nation be a beacon of Your light to the world.

In Jesus' Name, I pray. Amen.

A Prayer for Parents

Heavenly Father,

I thank You for the gift of parents and the incredible responsibility You've entrusted to them. Today, I lift up all parents to Your loving care, asking for Your wisdom, strength and guidance as they nurture and raise their children.

Lord, grant parents the patience and grace they need to face the daily challenges of parenting. Help them to lead by example, modeling Christ-like love, humility and integrity in their homes. Equip them with the wisdom to make decisions that align with Your will and the courage to stand firm in their faith.

Father, bless parents with hearts filled with love and compassion, even during difficult seasons. Teach them to pray for and with their children, planting seeds of faith that will bear fruit for generations to come. Comfort those who may feel overwhelmed or inadequate, reminding them that Your grace is sufficient and You are always near.

Strengthen families with unity, understanding and forgiveness, drawing them closer to one another and to You. May every parent rely on Your Word as their guide, trusting in Your promises and provision for their families.

In Jesus' Name, I pray. Amen.

A Prayer for Our School Children

Heavenly Father,

I come before You with grateful hearts, lifting up our school children to Your loving care. Thank You for the gift of education and for the teachers, staff and parents who nurture their growth. I ask for Your divine protection over each child as they travel to and from school, walk the halls and sit in their classrooms. Guard their hearts and minds from harm and shield them from danger seen and unseen.

Lord, fill our children with wisdom, understanding and a thirst for knowledge. Bless them with focus, discipline and the ability to learn and grow in excellence. Help them to remain kind and respectful to their peers and teachers, demonstrating the love of Christ in their actions. Surround them with positive influences and godly friends who will encourage them in righteousness.

I pray for those who may struggle academically, emotionally, or socially. Comfort them, Lord and provide the support they need to overcome challenges. Plant Your Word deeply in their hearts, that they may know You and trust in Your plans for their lives.

May they shine as lights in the world, bringing glory to Your Name. In Jesus' mighty Name, I pray. Amen.

WRITTEN BY:

Dr. Brenda Sawyer

INTERNATIONAL BEST-SELLING AUTHOR EDUCATIOR & SPEAKER

Dr. Brenda Sawyer, a Native New Yorker comes from humble beginnings and currently resides in Philadelphia with her daughter Natia. She is a retired educator, international best-selling author of Encouraging Words For The Mind, Spirit And Soul and an inspirational speaker. As a mentoring strategist and The Write Way Coach©, Dr. Sawyer's passion is to impart knowledge to individuals, unlock their potential through guidance and encouragement.

Dr. Sawyer holds a second Master's Degree in Elementary Education and holds an Honorary Doctorate Degree in Christian Humanities. She is the Founder and CEO of GIRLS WALKING WITH INTEGRITY EMPOWERING FOR DESTINY (GWWI)®, where she mentors and equips Christian women ages 45-65 to transform their lives through Biblical principles and teaching, while leaving an indelible legacy for posterity and confidence.

Additionally, Dr. Sawyer heads God Wants To Get The Glory From Your Story© where she hosts Zoom interviews for individuals to share their stories of faith and miracles. When she is not mentoring, coaching, being featured in magazines, antholgies and being a guest on podcasts, you can find her on Clubhouse for inspiring faith-building sessions such as TESTIMONY TUESDAY and The Power of The Tongue.

Dr. Sawyer can be contacted at, brendasawyer084@gmail.com or on Instagram at brendasawyerencourages

- (f) brendasawyer.58
- (ig) @brendasawyerencourages
- (🌐) brendasawyer.com

God Meets Every Need

"LET EVERYTHING THAT HAS BREATH PRAISE THE LORD! PRAISE THE LORD!"
(PSALM 150:6)

I Looked In A Different Mirror

Most Gracious and Holy Father,

I come before You with a heart full of gratitude, thankful for the new vision You have given me. I praise You for how You see me—not just as I am, but as I can be through Your grace and love. Father, help me to embrace the truth that I am fearfully and wonderfully made, a designer's original crafted in Your image.

Thank You for this moment and the continued moments of clarity when I recognize my worth is not defined by the world. May I always remember that I am cherished and valued, deserving of joy and peace.

As I face life's challenges, give me the strength to see myself through the reflection of your word. Appreciating my strengths and acknowledging my weaknesses without shame. Let Your light shine through me, reminding me that I am worthy of forgiveness and capable of growth.

I ask for the wisdom to extend this same vision to others, seeing them as You see them. Let my heart overflow with gratitude as I walk this journey, continually reminded of Your love towards me. In your matchless name, I pray.

Amen.

I Trust You With It All

Most Gracious and Holy Father,

I come before You today with a heart full of gratitude and trust. Your Word in 1st Peter 5:7 teaches me to cast all my cares upon You, for You care for me. So today and forever, I trust you with it all! I surrender my worries, anxieties, and burdens to You.

I place my faith in Your loving hands, knowing You are always near, ready to comfort and guide me. Fill my heart with Your peace, which surpasses all understanding. Remind me daily that Your grace is sufficient, and Your love is unwavering.

Thank You for Your constant care and for being my refuge. Help me walk in faith and not fear, because you are always in control. I thank You for Your presence being my strength and Your promises my hope. I trust you with it all!

In Jesus' name, I pray. Amen.

I Am Worth It!

Most Gracious and Holy Father,

I am amazed that you thought I was worth Sending Your only Son into the world to give His life so that I might have eternal life through Him. This incredible gift is proof of Your unwavering love for me.

Lord, sometimes my vision is clouded by the world's perception, making it hard for me to see my worth and value. But help me to remember Your Word say that I am fearfully and wonderfully made.

Lord, help me to see myself through Your eyes. Remind me of the gifts and qualities You have given me. Remind me that I am Your beloved child, created with purpose. Strengthen my heart and mind so that I may reject any lies that tell me otherwise. Fill me with Your peace and confidence, knowing that my worth is not determined by the world but by You.

Help me to walk in the truth of who I am in You. Guide me to live out my potential and to embrace the beauty within me. Thank You for Your love and for always seeing my worth, even when I struggle to.

In Jesus' name, I pray. Amen.

I Am Whole!

Most Gracious and Holy Father,

Today, humbly come to You, acknowledging that in Christ, I am made complete. Colossians 2:10 reminds me that I have been filled in Him, who is the Lord over every power and authority.

Lord, help me to truly understand and embrace this completeness. In moments of doubt, remind me that I am whole in You. Fill my heart with the confidence that I lack nothing because of Your grace and love.

Help me to live out this truth daily! I Am Whole! Let Your fullness within me be evident in my actions, words, and thoughts. Strengthen me to walk in conviction, knowing that You are my source of all strength and wisdom.

Thank You, Lord, for making me complete in Christ. Be my guiding light, and Your truth be my foundation.

In Jesus' name, I pray. Amen.

I Am in the Right Posture to Learn!

Most Gracious and Holy Father,

I come before You today with a heart eager to receive Your wisdom and understanding. I pray that You fill my heart with the fear of the Lord this is the first step to obtaining your wisdom.

Lord, help me to incline my ear to wisdom and apply my heart to understanding. May I sincerely seek Your wisdom and understanding, knowing that they are more precious than silver and hidden treasures.

Give me the discernment to recognize and value the knowledge You impart, Lord, and open my mind to Your truths as I cry aloud for knowledge.

Thank You, Lord, for the promise that when I seek Your wisdom with a sincere heart, I will understand and find the knowledge of God. Lord, guide my path and lead me closer to You each day. In Jesus' name, I pray.

WRITTEN BY:

Minister Karen Lynn Morton

MINISTER

Karen Lynn Morton is a multifaceted individual who has successfully worked in both the public and private sectors. Lynn is a minister, certified coach, speaker, trainer, and Entrepreneur. She is the founder and CEO of K. L. Morton Enterprises and the founder and executive director of The Woman of God's Design Ministry. One of Lynn's areas of work is Restorative Justice where she specializes in training parents, teachers, and school program development.

Because of this work, The Balanced and Restorative Justice (BARJ) Taskforce of the Cook County Juvenile Court honored Lynn as one of its 2011 awardees. Lynn's expertise has been called upon by the City of Chicago Office of Violence Prevention as well as local and national Universities and organizations to speak and/or train in Restorative Justice in Schools and community. Lynn has also received an executive appointment to the Illinois Recess in Schools Taskforce.

Lynn is a graduate of Robert Morris College with a degree in Computerized Business Systems/Accounting. She is a John Maxwell certified trainer, speaker, and coach. She is the proud mother of one son, Stephan Morton. Stephan is a college graduate and an entrepreneur who loves to worship.

 karen.l.morton.73 and WOGDMINISTRY

God Is Our Shepherd

"THE LORD IS MY SHEPHERD; I SHALL NOT WANT. HE MAKES ME LIE DOWN IN GREEN PASTURES. HE LEADS ME BESIDE STILL WATERS."
(PSALM 23:1-2)

Faith in Uncertain Times

Lord, thank you for allowing us to walk by faith, not by sight. Please help us have faith during these uncertain times. Help us remember that there is always certainty in you. We are fully aware that you are our real source.

As we acknowledge and put you first, thank you for ordering our steps towards our future. Our path is clear, and we will not stumble or fall as we keep our eyes on you. Please help us accept the process for our purpose. Every step, moment, instance, setback, and victory counts towards our destiny.

Thank you for helping us know our place in the Kingdom and that you keep our feet steady and sure. Please help us be stable while we go through the trials that prepare us to fulfill our purpose here.

Thank you that we understand that faith comes by hearing and hearing Your word. Even when things are hard, please help us know that the trials we go through right now are not the final decisions of the future.

Please help us understand that the past is gone; we will move through these uncertain times while the future is in our view.

Overcomers

Father, thank you that we overcome by the blood of the Lamb and by the Word of our testimony. Please help us to make wise decisions that are determined by listening to the voice of your Spirit. Thank you for the victory over sin and death. Thank you that no weapons formed against us shall be able to prosper and that every tongue that rises against us in judgment shall be shown to be in the wrong. Validate us before our enemies and help us walk as overcomers. Please help us maintain a stance worthy of being called children of the Kingdom. Please help us step up to Kingdom principles and flee from the world's influence.

Thank you for making our name great all over the land. Thank you for using our favor and influence to draw people to you so they can see your goodness in the land of the living. We are no longer your enemies when we choose Jesus, but we are your dear children, and we accept the victory that Jesus, our brother, won.

Please help us show our overcoming nature by standing in faith. We believe you for victory in all areas of our lives.

Provision

Thank you for the provision that you have available to us. We release our lives into your hands so you can order our steps. You are our true source, and every resource and provision comes to us from you through others. Please help us walk out all that you have for us to walk out. We need to consult your Word repeatedly for our safety and security.

Our weapons are not carnal but mighty through you, God, to the pulling down of strongholds. Thank you, God, for being the source of our supply. Thank you that we accept and face every assignment in our lives. Even when trials come and distractions are intense, please help us maintain our desire to do what you have called us to do. Strengthen us in our inner man. Thank you for the grace to succeed when others plan our demise or failure.

Please help us to have strength in the face of the storm. Thank you for helping us know what road to take and what decisions to make. Please help us to recognize your provision for us in whatever form it comes.

Faithfulness

Lord God, you have been nothing but good and kind to us. Great is your faithfulness, God unto us. Thank You for continuing to unveil the secrets of your Word and the true meaning of what you have for us to do in life as we grow with you. Thank you for sticking with us even when we were against you. Thank you for loving us enough to send us your son Jesus.

Help us recognize that we received the love you shared while we were sinners. Please help us get past what people do so that we can help them have a relationship with you. Sustain us in our work for the Kingdom.

Thank you for extending your faithfulness to those who do not know you yet. Thank you for wishing that none should perish but that all should come to repentance. Because of your faithfulness to us, we pray that when we stand before your throne, we hear, well done, my good and faithful servant.

Extravagant Giving

F ather, move our hearts toward extravagant giving. Please help us to be generous as we listen to the voice of the Holy Spirit, leading and guiding us to all truth. Help us redefine how we look at the money and things we have obtained. Please help us to shift our thinking when it pertains to giving.

When prompted, we will show how awesome you have been to us and how great you can be to others. Help us to be your hands and heart on this earth. Help us not judge someone's situation and decide not to give because of what we think is happening in their lives or what they need or don't need. Help our extravagant giving tie directly to our obedience. You said that if we are willing and obedient, we will eat the good of the land.

When we feel prompted to give, please help us to answer the call. Please help us give until it seems extreme. Help others with our blessings in their hands to release them to us as we release what you have for us to share with others.

WRITTEN BY:

Dr. Jennifer Semien-Walker
DOCTOR OF BUSINESS ADMINISTRATION

Dr. Jennifer Semien-Walker, affectionately known as "Dr. Jenn," has dedicated over three decades to ministry. She served as a lay counselor, providing guidance and support to those in need.

Expanding her reach, Dr. Jenn has become a leader in social media ministry, connecting with and mentoring individuals globally through digital platforms.

One of Dr. Jenn's primary missions is to empower women to achieve their fullest potential. She aims to inspire women to embrace their strengths, overcome challenges, and strive for excellence in all aspects of their lives.

Her work continues to make a significant impact, touching lives and helping women around the world become the best versions of themselves.

- 🌐 renewedlivinginc.com
- ⓕ www.linkedin.com/in/jennifermsemien
- 🔗 www.facebook.com/jenniferm.semien

God Is Our Peace

"PEACE I LEAVE WITH YOU; MY PEACE I GIVE TO YOU. NOT AS THE WORLD GIVES DO I GIVE TO YOU. LET NOT YOUR HEARTS BE TROUBLED, NEITHER LET THEM BE AFRAID."
(JOHN 14:27)

To Be Like You

Heavenly Father,

I thank You for Your unwavering goodness and mercy. I desire to embody Your character in all aspects of my life. Help me to walk in Your ways, speak with Your kindness, and pray with fervor. Let Your Word dwell richly in my heart, guiding my thoughts and actions.

When I face challenges, remind me that Your joy is my strength. Be my shield in battles, and help me to look to You for guidance and support. Grant me a mind filled with peace, so that I may navigate my life with confidence in Your promises.

May my life reflect Your light, so that others may see Your glory shining through me. Help me to be worthy of Your righteousness, standing firm in my faith and purpose. In Jesus' name, I pray.

Amen.

I Trust You

Lord, please place your loving arms around me. Cover me with your peace and wipe my tears away. My heart is aching with an unspeakable pain.

My hope is knowing that you are close to my broken heart. My joy is knowing that you are my strength. When I am at my lowest, I look to the hills where all of my help comes from.

As I meditate on your word, I am able to get off of my face from grief and onto my knees in prayer, and mount up to my feet and continue to run my race without being weary.

In you Lord, I do trust. Amen.

I Give Thanks

Lord, I will bless You at all times;
Your praise shall continually be in my mouth.
I thank You for my life—every breath, every moment, a gift from You.
I thank You for my strength, renewed by Your power.
I thank You for my family, a blessing and a reflection of Your love.
I thank You for Your glory, which fills the heavens and the earth.
I thank You for Your never-ending mercies, fresh every morning.
I thank You for Your boundless love, which knows no limits.
I thank You for Your peace, which calms my heart in the midst of chaos.
I thank You for Your graciousness, showered upon me even when I fall short.
I thank You for Your blessings, seen and unseen.
I thank You for Your goodness, which follows me all the days of my life.
I thank You for Your forgiveness, which sets me free.
And most of all, I thank You for hanging on the cross for me,
paying the ultimate price so that I might live in Your grace.
With all that I am, I give You glory and honor,
today and forevermore.
In Jesus' name, Amen.

Gracious God

Every day when I open my eyes, I am overwhelmed with gratitude for the new day You have granted me. Each breath I take is a reminder of Your mercy and love—a fresh chance to live my life for You.

Lord, I dedicate every moment to You. With every chance I have, I will proclaim Your glory and tell of Your wondrous works. May my words and actions honor You, drawing others to Your light and truth.

Thank You for being my guide, my strength, and my purpose. Let my life reflect Your love, and may everything I do bring glory to Your name.

In Jesus' name, Amen.

Use Me, Lord

Heal me, O Lord, that I might be healed.
Save me, O Lord, that I might be saved.
For You alone are my hope, my refuge, and my strength.
If I could just touch the hem of Your garment,
I know I would be restored by Your glory.
And when I receive Your healing touch,
I will proclaim Your name to the world,
so that others may see You through me.
Let the words I speak bring hope and truth,
drawing hearts closer to You.
Use me, Lord, as a vessel of Your love and light.
May my life testify of Your power and grace,
bringing glory to Your name forevermore.
In Jesus' name,
Amen.

WRITTEN BY:

Patrice Head

DEDICATED EDUCATOR

Patrice Head is a dedicated educator with over 20 years of experience specializing in Special Education. Her passion for teaching and commitment to empowering students with diverse needs led her to earn a Specialist Degree in Special Education from Northcentral University.

Throughout her career, Patrice has made a significant impact in the lives of her students, fostering an inclusive and supportive learning environment.

Beyond her professional endeavors, Patrice is actively involved in her church community, where she has taken on various leadership roles. Her contributions include serving as the assistant Sunday School secretary, choir president, church announcer, trustee, food bank coordinator, and assistant financial clerk. Through these roles, Patrice demonstrates her strong commitment to service, collaboration, and fostering a sense of community.

Patrice's unwavering dedication to education and community engagement reflects her belief in the transformative power of support and understanding, both in the classroom and beyond.

God Is Our Protector

"THE LORD WILL KEEP YOU FROM ALL EVIL; HE WILL KEEP YOUR LIFE. THE LORD WILL KEEP YOUR GOING OUT AND YOUR COMING IN FROM THIS TIME FORTH AND FOREVERMORE."
(PSALM 121:7-8)

Prayer for Renewed Strength

Grant us the strength to rise above challenges, to embrace each day with renewed hope and determination.

Let our hearts be fortified with courage and resilience, knowing that every step forward brings us closer to healing.

May we find comfort in the knowledge that even in our weakest moments, You are carrying us, guiding us toward wholeness.

Bless our bodies with vitality, our spirits with perseverance, and our minds with peace.

Amen.

Prayer for Family Unity

Thank You for the gift of family, the cornerstone of love and connection. Strengthen the bonds that unite us, even through challenges.

Help us to communicate with kindness, forgive freely, and celebrate each other's joys. May our home be a place of peace, laughter, and grace, reflecting love.

Bless each member of our family, guiding us to grow in faith and unity. Let the moments we share become cherished memories, deepening our connection and inspiring us to support and uplift one another.

Amen.

Prayer for Gratitude and Hope

Thank You for the blessings, both seen and unseen, that grace our lives each day. Teach us to live with gratitude, even in times of struggle, and to recognize the small miracles that surround us.

Fill our hearts with hope for the future, knowing that all is good and perfect. May we radiate this gratitude and hope to others, uplifting and inspiring them in their own journeys.

Amen.

Prayer for Wisdom in Healing

Bless us with the wisdom to listen to our bodies, to recognize the signs of imbalance, and to seek paths of healing.

Guide us to make choices that nurture health and vitality. Surround us with knowledge, support, and encouragement as we embrace transformation.

May Your divine wisdom inspire us to trust the process, to celebrate progress, and to cherish the journey toward wholeness.

Amen.

Prayer for Connection with Nature

Thank You for the gift of nature, a reflection and a source of endless healing. As we walk among trees, breathe the fresh air, and feel the warmth of the sun, may we be reminded of Your presence.

Let the rhythm of the waves, the songs of the birds, and the stillness of the forest restore our souls. Teach us to care for this Earth and to draw strength from its beauty.

Amen.

WRITTEN BY:

Elaine Gibson
HEALTHY LIFESTYLE DESIGNER

Elaine Gibson, founder of Renewed Living and creator of the Extraordinary Living Made Easy method, is a bestselling author, motivational speaker, workshop facilitator, private coach, and green juicing grandmother.

Named one of the world's top 10 natural cancer survivors by Extreme Health Radio (#4), Elaine overcame Stage IV cancer without traditional protocols.

Facing death inspired her to embrace life fully. She shares her hard-won wisdom for creating a disease-free lifestyle and longevity, helping women with cancer reclaim vitality and wellness—without giving up chocolate.

Elaine envisions a world where cancer is just a chapter, not the whole story.

🌐 renewedlivinginc.com

God Is Ever-Present

"GOD IS OUR REFUGE AND STRENGTH, A VERY
PRESENT HELP IN TROUBLE."
(PSALM 46:1)

A Prayer To Ascend

Heavenly Father, we come before you right now, thanking you, praising you, honoring you, worshipping you, praising you, for your grace, favor and mercy. We thank you for just being our sovereign God and sharing your throne with none, which is a sweet reminder that despite what it may look like or feel like, the enemy nor our enemies are in control.

Lord, as we humble ourselves before you, we thank you that we can trust your word that says, "all things work together for our good," Romans 8:28.

So, as we stand on your word, help us to remember, anything you have allowed, is working for us and not against us.

Help us be reminded of Jesus, who after His crucifixion, Matthew 28:19 records, He got up with all power and authority in His Hands.

Help us to remember to allow Him to serve as our reminder and example, that power comes after perseverance and that anything we survive, we now have authority over. Like Joseph, help us to trust you to transmute everything the enemy meant for evil into a force that helps us to rise for the greater good, our purpose, your purpose, our destiny, call, purpose and assignment. Help us to not get weary while we wait on you to help us come back from everything the enemy was sure would bury us.

Help us to remember, that like Jesus, we too shall ascend.

In your precious son Jesus name we pray, it is so and amen!

Healing For Your Emotions

Father God, we come before you right now, asking for a healing that only you can provide. Touch the emotions of everyone reading right now. Help us to remember that no pain is too big or too small for your Holy Spirit to minister to. Soothe our emotions as only you can.

Be a Balm in Gilead to every wounded place.

Cause Your Holy Spirit to heal, recover, mend every broken place in us, quickly. Let us not have to toil in anguish much longer.

Lord, get into the "aches" of the situation as only you can. Every place that we feel the pain of any emotion, the residue of any experience that hurt us, touch it, heal it. Don't allow pain to take over us and become our everyday reality or identity.

May we feel your power more than we feel the pain of what happened. May a calm begin to take over us right now, that gives us hope that we can survive what feels so intense right now. Give us a peace that surpasses understanding.

May the power of your Holy Spirit wash over us right now like waves from the ocean, touching every place in us, renewing a sense of peace and joy. Help us to believe that brighter days are coming.

Help us to replace any despair, with hope.

In Jesus name we pray, Amen.

Healing For Your Womb

Father God, we come before you right now, asking you to enter our wombs and make everything wrong, right.

Ease all pain, correct any diagnosis, cause us to be well, fruitful and multiply. Cause us to be whole, inside and out, as you fully intended. Let no diagnosis or pain reign over us.

Help us to remember that Jesus was crucified, so we can be well and by His stripes we are healed.

Help us to walk in the knowing of your power, that doctors practice, but you perform!

Right now, we invite your healing hands into our life, into our body, into our womb, to do what only you can do.

We thank you that we believe by the power of your might, we are healed! We thank you that we believe it is by your power, we are set free from any suffering. We thank you, that like the woman with the issue of blood, we believe, we are well because you have the power to cause it to be so.

Help us to hold on to our faith in you, until we can testify, we are healed!

In Jesus name we pray, Amen.

Healing For Your Focus

Father God, we come before you right now, asking you to help us to focus more. We know we have an assignment, call, purpose and destiny to fulfill. Help us to do so!

Give us the discipline to cast down imaginations, the spirit of procrastination and anything that so easily comes to distract us, delay us and keep us from staying focused on the tasks you have assigned us.

Lord, we lay our focus at the altar and ask that you increase it. May our lack of focus, no longer be a weapon that the enemy can use to stop our progression.

Be a mind regulator!

Help us to be like Nehemiah and get the job done, no matter any distraction.

Sharpen our focus. Renew our drive. Increase our commitment and discipline to finish tasks you have set before us.

Lord, help us to no longer find joy or comfort in procrastinating. May we find joy and peace in staying focused.

In Jesus name we pray, Amen.

Healing For Your Energy

Father God, we come before you right now, asking you to increase our energy. Lord, we confess at times we feel weary, downtrodden, overtaken, unable to progress like we should.

Sometimes, we feel like the very life has been sucked out of us.

We know this is not your will.

Be it our eating habits, lack of proper rest, whatever the cause may be, uncover it to us and give us the strength we need to no longer feel depleted.

Touch our bodies and minds right now. Help us to not be a slave to how we feel but to have enough energy to override how we feel to do what needs to be done to complete the tasks before us. Give us the energy to get up and get active, get moving towards our goals, our purpose, our assignment, our destiny.

May we no longer be held captive to not having enough energy. Help us to remember the power of the Holy Spirit, which lives in us, our resource who gives us the strength that we need.

We bind up the spirit of heaviness, the spirit of depression, the spirit of delay and anything else that may be hindering our feeling like we have the ability to get moving.

In Jesus name we pray, Amen.

WRITTEN BY:

Tera Carissa Hodges

CERTIFIED WOMEN'S LIFE COACH AND EMPOWERMENT SPEAKER

A verifiable 7 figure earning certified women's life coach and empowerment speaker, Tera Carissa Hodges has been featured in Essence, Yahoo Finance, Hype Magazine and more, has participated as the keynote speaker at women's empowerment events sponsored by Mercedes Benz, JP Morgan and more.

Currently, her greeting card line through Culture Greetings is available at Walgreens and is a featured authored in internationally renowned speaker, Les Brown's latest book, Your Story Sells and Volume 1 of Percy "Master P" Miller's, Mastering Wealth.

A philanthropist at heart, she's built wells in Nigeria and supplies fresh water systems in Zimbabwe.

A licensed and ordained minister, her prayer for corporate women has been featured in Essence Magazine. She's also provided voice overs for the audio companion to The Bible Experience which aired on The History Channel, produced by Mark Burnett, creator of The Apprentice, Shark Tank and more and Roma Downey, from Touched By An Angel.

An advocate for women, she has trademarked and launched Success Bullying to help successful women navigate jealousy and hate aimed at disparaging them because of their success.

A moderator for the 79th United Nations General Assembly Science Summit, she also leads an empowerment teleconference line where she serves over 10,000 people weekly in over 30 countries.

 www.teracarissa.com

God Is All-Powerful

"AH, LORD GOD! IT IS YOU WHO HAVE MADE
THE HEAVENS AND THE EARTH BY YOUR
GREAT POWER AND BY YOUR OUTSTRETCHED
ARM! NOTHING IS TOO HARD FOR YOU."
(JEREMIAH 32:17)

Pray First

Abba Father,

I come before You with an open heart, ready to align with Your will. Thank You for being my guide, my strength, and my ever-present help in every season of life. I acknowledge that without You, I can do nothing, but through You, I can do all things.

Lord, forgive me for the times I've trusted in others or my own understanding instead of placing my trust fully in You. Thank You for the discipline to seek You first, and help me to always turn to You before anyone or anything else. Open my eyes to see You clearly in every situation and guide my steps with Your wisdom.

I ask for clarity and courage as I seek to fulfill the purpose You have placed within me. Stir up the gifts You've deposited in my heart and let me not be paralyzed by fear, doubt, or uncertainty.

Father, let my prayers be my foundation and my actions the evidence of my faith. Empower me to move with intention, trusting that You will order my steps as I walk forward. May my life reflect Your glory and inspire others to seek You first in all things.

In Jesus Name, Amen

A Prayer of Healing and Surrender to the Lord

Heavenly Father,

Thank You for this day that You have made. Thank You for the gift of a new day, filled with new mercies and abundant grace. Thank You for keeping and protecting me, for surrounding me with Your angels who have charge over me. Thank You for Your goodness and mercy that follow me all the days of my life. I praise You for Your promises that are yes and amen, and for the breath of life that sustains me. Thank You, Lord, for Your Word, a lamp to my feet and a light to my path, guiding me daily in truth and love.

Today, I surrender my whole self to You. I lift my body, mind, and spirit into Your hands, asking that Your healing virtue flow through me from the crown of my head to the soles of my feet. I thank You that I am healed, whole, and restored by the power of Jesus Christ. I command my blood, cells, organs, and every system in my body to function as You perfectly designed.

I declare that I am healed, I am whole, I am delivered, and I am set free. Thank You, Father, for hearing my prayer and for Your faithfulness.

In Jesus' name, Amen.

Surrendering Thoughts to God's Perfect Peace

Heavenly Father,

Thank You for this day that You have made. Thank You for the gift of a sound mind and the peace that surpasses all understanding. Thank You for Your Word, which renews my thoughts and transforms my life. Thank You for being my protector, my keeper, and the anchor of my soul. I am grateful for Your promises that are yes and amen, and for the strength and clarity You provide in every moment.

Today, I surrender my mind to You. I ask that You cleanse and purify my thoughts. Let Your healing virtue flow through every corner of my mind, bringing peace where there is confusion, hope where there is despair, and joy where there is heaviness. I rebuke every lie of the enemy and replace it with the truth of Your Word. I declare that my thoughts are aligned with Your will, and my mind operates in the fullness of Your design.

I thank You, Lord, that I am healed in my mind. I am renewed, I am whole, I am delivered, and I am set free. Thank You for hearing my prayer and for leading me into a place of perfect peace.

In Jesus' name, Amen.

Finding Strength and Hope in God's Unfailing Promises

Abba Father,

Thank You for this day that You have made. Thank You for being close to the brokenhearted and for Your unfailing love that never leaves me. I praise You for Your promises that are true, for Your comfort that soothes my soul, and for the hope You bring to every situation. Thank You for being my refuge and my strength, my ever-present help in times of trouble.

Today, I surrender my broken heart to You. I ask that You pour out Your healing virtue and bind up every wound. Take the pieces of my heart and restore them with Your love, grace, and peace. Help me release the pain, disappointment, and sorrow into Your hands, trusting that You are working all things together for my good.

Lord, fill the empty spaces with Your presence, replacing grief with joy, hurt with hope, and despair with renewed purpose. I declare that my heart is whole, healed, and free. Thank You for being the lifter of my head and the healer of my soul.

I thank You for Your faithfulness and for hearing my prayer. I walk in the confidence of Your love and restoration.

In Jesus' name, Amen.

Trusting God's Faithfulness in the Journey of Motherhood

Gracious God,

Thank You for this day and for Your steadfast love and faithfulness. Thank You for being the source of life, strength, and hope. I praise You for Your promises that are true and for Your unfailing grace that sustains me in every season. Thank You for the precious life growing within me and for Your hand upon this journey.

Today, I lift my heart and my body to You as I walk through this high-risk pregnancy. Lord, I ask for Your divine protection over me and my baby. Cover us with Your healing virtue and keep every system in our bodies functioning as You designed. Strengthen me physically, emotionally, and spiritually to face each day with courage and peace.

Help me to release fear, anxiety, and uncertainty into Your hands, trusting that You are the Great Physician and the Giver of life. Surround me with Your presence and remind me of Your power to do all things well.

I declare that both my baby and I are safe, healthy, and surrounded by Your perfect love. Thank You for Your faithfulness, for hearing my prayers, and for walking this journey with me.

It is so - In Jesus' name, Amen.

WRITTEN BY:

Marcella D. Moore
ELDER, FOUNDER AND CEO

Marcella D. Moore is a transformational speaker, empowerment coach, author, and founder of Motivate and Pray, Inc., an empowerment and prayer ministry. She serves as a Servant Leader at Abundant Life Family Worship Church, where she oversees the Seniors Ministry.

A recipient of numerous industry awards, Marcella's work reflects her dedication to excellence and impact.

Passionate about prayer, personal development, and uplifting others, she inspires people to "be a part of your own rescue" by embracing their unique gifts, living purposefully, and making a difference in their communities.

 marcelladmoore.com

God Is Love

"SO WE HAVE COME TO KNOW AND TO
BELIEVE THE LOVE THAT GOD HAS FOR US.
GOD IS LOVE, AND WHOEVER ABIDES IN LOVE
ABIDES IN GOD, AND GOD ABIDES IN HIM."
(1 JOHN 4:16)

Anointed Hands: A Prayer for Purposeful Work

Mighty El Shaddai, I come before You with a humble heart, lifting my hands to You in prayer. These hands that You have crafted with such precision are meant for useful work. I prepare them daily and diligently to serve You and others. At the beginning of each day, I anoint my hands with oil for purpose and pray for Your anointing to be upon them. Let them be instruments of Your peace and love. Let everything, they touch be blessed.

As my hands are lifted in a position of surrender, it signifies my total relinquishment to You. This is how I fight my battles. You do Your best work when I open my hands. May they build where there has been destruction, give where there is need, and comfort where there is sorrow. My hands, when lifted, offer You praise, acknowledging the Great "I AM." In times of stillness, may my hands fold in prayer, connecting with You, seeking Your wisdom and grace. And in times of action, may they reach out to give and to heal.

I entrust my hands to Your care, asking for protection against any diseases or injuries that may afflict them. Bless my hands with health and strength, that they may perform the work You have set before me with skill and grace. "The works of His hands are faithful and just; all His precepts are trustworthy" (Psalm 111:7). Let my hands reflect Your faithfulness in every task and keep them from harm, so they can continue to serve Your purpose.

In the name of Lord Jesus,
Amen.

Pathfinder's Blessing: A Prayer for Guided Steps

Heavenly Father, I lift my feet to You in prayer, asking that You guide each step I take. Bless my feet as they tread through varying paths of life. Grant them the strength to stand firm in faith and the agility to move with grace and purpose. Protect them from the stumbles of life and lead me to walk in the ways of Your truth and love. May my journey always bring me closer to You, and may my footprints leave a legacy of kindness and good faith.

Lord, protect them from harm and disease as they walk through life's journey. Guard them from all ailments that may try to hinder my steps, whether emotional, spiritual, or physical. Strengthen them to carry me towards acts of goodness and mercy. "How beautiful are the feet of those who bring good news!" (Romans 10:15). May my feet always be a testament to Your path of peace and Your good news.

In the name of our precious Lord Jesus,
Amen.

Strength to Stand: A Prayer for Back Support

Almighty God, help me to carry my burdens wisely, leaning on Your everlasting arms when the load is too heavy. Fortify my core with Your spiritual and physical resilience, enabling me to stand upright and face the challenges of each day with courage and endurance. May I support others as You support me, with strength and love.

I pray for the well-being of my back, that You may shield it from injuries and diseases such as strains or chronic pain. Grant relief from the pain and strain that I endure. Help me to carry my burdens with the strength provided by Your grace.

"The Lord is my strength and my shield; my heart trusts in Him, and He helps me" (Psalm 28:7). Let this strength be the support of my back, enabling me to stand tall and face each day with renewed vigor.

In the glorious name of Jesus Christ,
Amen.

Crown of Clarity: A Prayer for Intellectual Illumination

Creator of All, I thank You for the gift of my brain, the center of my thought and reason. I pray for clarity of mind, creativity, and calmness that surpasses all understanding. Protect my mind from confusion and doubt and bless me with wisdom and insight. May my thoughts be pleasing to You, focused on truth, and guided by Your light. Empower my brain to learn, grow, and adapt, so I may solve the problems I face and discover new ways to honor You in all I do.

Guard my mind against any disorders or diseases. Endow my brain with health and vitality for clear thinking and decision-making.

"For God has not given us a spirit of fear, but of power and of love and of a sound mind" (2 Timothy 1:7). Protect my mental faculties, so I may use them to glorify You and serve those around me effectively.

In the glorious name of Jesus Christ,
Amen.

Foundation of Faith: A Prayer for Resilient Knee

Gracious Lord, I bow my knees in reverence and ask for Your blessings upon them. As I kneel in prayer and rise to meet the demands of the day, strengthen my knees to endure. Let my knees remind me of the power of bending in humility and standing in faith. May they carry me through life's journey, always bending in prayer and standing for what is right.

I ask for Your divine protection over my knees. Heal any pain that hinders me and provide the flexibility and stability needed to walk, run, and rest. Shield them from ailments such as arthritis or injury that can impair their function. Strengthen and heal them, enabling me to move in service to Your will.

"The Lord is my strength and my song; He has become my salvation" (Psalm 118:14). May I always find the strength in You to rise from my knees in prayer and step forward in faith.

In the name of Lord Jesus,
Amen.

WRITTEN BY:

Sharon Baker

COACH AND CONSULTANT

Sharon Baker, founder of Embracing Abundance Life Coaching, boasts over 25 years of expertise as a certified business professional and life coach. Renowned for her transformative impact in the corporate sector, she excels in training, development, and employee engagement.

Sharon's approach seamlessly combines business acumen with innovative coaching techniques, empowering individuals and organizations alike. As a training consultant, she partners with organizations to cultivate resilient workforces and environments rich in creativity and teamwork.

An acclaimed speaker and author, Sharon has been featured in top publications and received the Presidential Lifetime Achievement Award for her extensive volunteer work and societal contributions.

 embracingabundancelifecoaching.com

God Is Merciful

"THE LORD IS MERCIFUL AND GRACIOUS,
SLOW TO ANGER AND ABOUNDING IN
STEADFAST LOVE."
(PSALM 103:8)

A Prayer for Inner Healing and Transformation

Heavenly Father,

We come before You, grateful for Your love that heals and transforms. Thank You for guiding us on this journey of manifesting inner healing through Your divine Agape love. Lord, we acknowledge the broken places within us, the voids we've carried for too long. We release them to You now, knowing that only You can fill the emptiness with Your grace and purpose.

As we walk this path of healing, teach us to embrace vulnerability. Strip away the masks we've worn and help us stand before You, unashamed and free. Let Your truth saturate our hearts, renewing our minds and restoring our spirits. Lord, ignite in us the boldness to share our testimonies of victory, so that others may see Your power at work within us.

We pray for every woman seeking healing and wholeness. Let Your love remind them that they are seen, valued, and called to a higher purpose. Give them the courage to step out of the shadows of their past and into the light of Your plan for their lives. May we all walk in the fullness of Your healing, knowing that in You, we are whole.

In Jesus' name, Amen

A Prayer for Healing Through Forgiveness

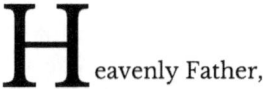

Heavenly Father,

Thank You for the gift of forgiveness. I come before You with a heart open to release every weight of bitterness, pain, and regret. I recognize that true healing comes through the power of forgiveness, a gift You have freely given through Jesus. Lord, I ask for the strength to forgive not only those who have wronged me but also myself. In letting go of past hurts, I open my heart to the restoration You promise.

Thank You, Jesus, for bearing the weight of my sins and for showing me the path to grace. I declare that, through Your sacrifice, I am made whole. I am empowered to walk forward in freedom, no longer chained to the wounds of the past. With each step, I embrace the new You have prepared for me, surrendering every painful memory into Your loving hands.

Renew my mind, Father, and help me to see myself through Your eyes. May I live out the purpose You've placed in me, healed and whole. I praise You for Your mercy and for teaching me to love myself as You love me.

In Jesus' name, Amen

Beauty in the Scars: A Prayer of Gratitude and Healing

F ather God,

I come before You, grateful for the scars I carry, for they tell a story of Your love and healing power in my life. Thank You for transforming my pain into purpose and my wounds into testimonies of Your faithfulness. Where the world sees weakness, I see strength, for my scars are proof of battles won through Your grace and mercy.

Lord, help me to embrace these marks, not with shame or fear, but with gratitude. Each scar tells of moments when I was tempted, accused, hurt, and broken, yet You never abandoned me. I am still here, standing as a witness of Your love, because I am Yours.

Let my scars be a light to others, a reminder of Your power to restore and redeem. Teach me to share my story openly, knowing that each mark is evidence of Jesus' victory in my life. I am chosen, healed, and whole in You. Thank You for loving me through every trial and for turning my brokenness into beauty.

In Jesus' name, Amen

A Prayer for Freedom and Renewed Purpose

Heavenly Father,

Thank You for Your grace that covers my past and renews my future. I come to You, laying down the burdens of my past mistakes, regrets, and pain. I know it's easy to feel trapped by memories and choices, but today, I choose to release them to You. I refuse to let my past dictate my present or hinder the future You have for me.

Lord, thank You for promising never to leave me nor forsake me. Your plans are filled with hope, purpose, and love, and I trust in Your divine guidance over my life. Teach me to see myself through Your eyes—a new creation in Christ, no longer bound by old mistakes. Help me to walk forward with confidence, free from guilt and shame.

Guide my heart, Father, as I make decisions aligned with Your will, unclouded by my past. Let my life reflect the hope and freedom that come from trusting in Your promises. Thank You for the future You have set before me, one filled with purpose, joy, and fulfillment in You.

In Jesus' name, Amen

A Prayer for Transformation and Surrender

Heavenly Father,

Thank You for the power of transformation at work in my life. I know this journey is not instant, but step-by-step, You are shaping me into the person You've called me to be. I surrender the unresolved issues of my past, trusting that You are using them as the foundation for a brighter future. Each struggle, each lesson, and each victory is a building block toward the promises You have set before me.

Lord, Your love surrounds me daily, reminding me to live with hope and anticipation for what lies ahead. Your grace gives me strength to face each day with faith, knowing that You are constantly working in and through me. My journey is my testimony, and I treasure it as evidence of Your goodness and faithfulness.

Help me to embrace each step with patience, knowing that every trial is shaping me for a greater purpose. Let my life shine as a witness to others of Your power to transform and redeem. I am grateful for this journey and for the promise of what's yet to come.

In Jesus' name, Amen

WRITTEN BY:

Mia Knight
CONTENT CREATOR, AUTHOR, AND SPEAKER

My name is Mia Knight, mother of three beautiful daughters and grandmother of 3 handsome little boys.

I am a content creator, author, and speaker with a heart for helping women heal from trauma and find purpose in their pain.

My journey of overcoming childhood trauma has shaped who I am today, and through my story, I aim to inspire others to break free from generational cycles and step into the fullness of their true identity. As the founder of She Is M-I-A (Manifesting Inner Healing through Agape), my mission is to empower women to experience inner healing through the transformative power of God's love. I've created a space where we can come together to share our stories, grow spiritually, and walk into the freedom that Christ offers.

In my books, Seeds of My Existence and Single, Saved, and Unfulfilled: Finding Me in Him, I explore themes of self-discovery, faith, and the victory that comes when we allow God to turn our pain into purpose. Through my writing, speaking, and online ministry, I'm dedicated to helping others reclaim their lives and experience the healing that leads to true freedom.

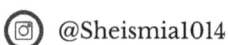 @Sheismia1014

God Is Righteous

"FOR THE LORD IS RIGHTEOUS; HE LOVES
RIGHTEOUS DEEDS; THE UPRIGHT SHALL
BEHOLD HIS FACE."
(PSALM 11:7)

Mending The Broken Pieces.

When dark clouds of doubt, weariness, defeat, pain and discouragement gather penetrate my soul with rays of Hope. Uphold me by your right hand according to your word Isaiah 41v10.

Thank you for your power that is perfected in my weakness 2 Corinthians 12 v9. Holy spirit fill me afresh with joy, peace, endurance and persevering strength.

Like David in 1 Samuel 30 v8 may I always enquire of the Lord according in the day of trouble and affliction without being discouraged and being weary. My rock and fortress I praise you.

In Deuteronomy 31 v8 Your word says you will never leave me nor forsake me, I thank you that when I'm down, forsaken, abandoned, mourning, betrayed, disappointed your goodness and mercy follow me all the days of my life. Forgive me for the times I questioned you, turned my back on you and doubted you about the circumstances in my life.

Teach me to trust in you whole heartdly so that I might find perfect peace in you as you promised in Isiah 26 v 3-4.

You Mountain Be Levelled Up

Lord I recognize your promises over our lives because you're a God of integrity and you have all abilities and power. God Almighty who is bigger than us. Jehovah mighty in battle.

My God who sees me even when I have reached the end of myself. I lift my voice before you ,Lord confront my confrontations and every prevailing forces rising against my life. Level every mountain before me. Isiah 45:2-3. Level mountains of poverty/wrong relationships/ignorance/depression/fear/sickness/untimely death/anti progress and stagnation in Jesus name.

Let every personal Jericho standing in front of me be uprooted in my life. Every mountain of pride be uprooted for Lord you despise the proud but give grace to the humble James 4:6-10. Thank you for enabling me to work on my faith for without faith it is impossible to please God and impossible to win battles Gal 6:7-9. Let every mountain become a plain (be removed) in my life and every valley brought low.

Thank you for granting me victory. I'm a winner in Jesus precious name Amen.

Courage and Resilience

Thank you Lord for encouraging me to be brave and courageous Joshua 1:9 for you are always with me. I am not afraid. You strengthen me and help me always Isa41:10. My steps are ordered by the Lord I submit myself to the plans and purposes of God Gal 6:9. I am crowned with Endurance and steadfastness in my heart I chose to stand trials. James 1:2 I am not afraid of my enemies for your rod and staff comfort me Ps 23:4 I'm steadfast in trials and you shall crown me James 1v2.

I am alert, courageous and firm in my faith 1 Cor 16:13. My heart is strengthened to overcame the world John 16:33.

All things work for my good. I chose to love God because I am called according to the purposes of God. Your plans prosper me, I am delivered from harm therefore I shall reach my expected end Jer29:11. I can do all things through Christ Jesus who strengthens Phil 4:13. You are my Lord, my strength, my defence, my salvation. I will praise you, Oh God of my fathers and I will exalt your name Exodus 15:2. Surely goodness and mercy follows me all the days of my life and I dwell in the house of the Lord forever. Ps 26:6.

In Jesus might name. Amen

Conquering Sickness

Father in the name of Jesus Christ. I lift your name on high. Thank you Jesus Christ for dying for my sins and conquering sickness and death for me to be made whole 1 Peter 2 v24 .

I declare my body is not an instrument of sickness and diseases because Christ dwells in my mortal body. I break and rebuke any sickness programmed in the heavens to operate against me in Jesus name Ephesians 6v12. I command every organ in my body to function normal. I curse sickness and disease out of my life and lineage. I banish you from my body and my bloodline in the name of Jesus Christ. I declare no more untimely death because divinity recides in me Psalm 118v7 . Jesus show others your healing power so that they may also be healed and walk in your fullness. I receive healing of my spirit to perfect health Proverbs 18v4. I receive healing of my mind, will and emotions from brokenness and disappointments .

By his stripes I'm healed . I'm delivered .I'm set free in Jesus Christ name .

Trust the Process

Jesus Christ is the same yesterday, today and tomorrow Hebrews 13v8 . Thank you for you changeth not. I believe in your word, your abilities and your strength.

Thank you for being trustworthy and reliable.Romans 4:21. I am fully persuaded that God has power to do what he has promised. Thank you for being truthful and keeping your promises over my life and destiny. Luke 1:45 Blessed is she who has believed that what the Lord has said to her will be accomplished! I challenge powers of darkness that stand on my way with boldness knowing that you said I must be strong and courageous at all times. Joshua 1v9 . Isaiah 46:10. He makes known the end from the beginning, from ancient times, what is still to come. The Lord says His purpose will stand, and He will do all that He pleases. My future is planned and my steps are ordered to victory. The Lord works strength in me. Thank you for your light and grace as I face tragic circumstances 1 Thessalonians 5v16-1.

Thank you for a good future ahead Jeremiah 29v11 for my life will never be stranded when you're with me. Thank you for fighting visible and invisible battles for me. I put my faith and trust in your promises for me.

Thank you father in Jesus name

WRITTEN BY:

Pastor Angela Chademunhu
PASTOR AND LIFE COACH

Angela Chademunhu is a Pastor by calling and professional life coach, she is also a graduate in IT. She is the founder of "Hope for Life Ministry"She is a dynamic preacher in this end time. She preaches a message of "Hope".

Her mandate is to bring hope to a hopeless generation. Her message to humanity is that there is a God in heaven who can help mankind and restore him giving him life , hope and a future.

She is also the founder of "women on her knees" a women prayer movement with women from different parts of the world with online and physically meetings to intercede for revival, salvation of souls, for nations, society, families and individuals with the aim to raise an army of women who can wail, travail and give birth to destinies in prayer. She started her ministry 15 years ago, it was during her experiences in the struggles of emerging in her pastoral calling as a young female pastor in a looked down upon environment that writing books was inspired. With the dream of breaking through her environment she found also a hidden writing gift in her to express thoughts and feelings. She is currently working on her debut solo work and an anthology. In a largely male dominated field as a young single female Pastor it has not been an easy journey for her.

She is a woman helped by God. She soldiers on with a vision to change the world and raise women who reflect the true image of God's purpose, the original intended purpose of God. She believes in a greater glory daily to become a better version for her achieved and conquered levels. The love of God compels her to be a Philanthropist in Zimbabwe Africa. Her work largely extensively deals with widowed women and poor women who can hardly feed or raise their children. She is also a life coach who helps women with emotional and spiritual support. She focuses on the development of a balanced healed person.

(f) Angela Chademunhu

God is Our Redeemer

"BUT NOW THUS SAYS THE LORD, HE WHO
CREATED YOU, O JACOB, HE WHO FORMED
YOU, O ISRAEL: 'FEAR NOT, FOR I HAVE
REDEEMED YOU; I HAVE CALLED YOU BY
NAME, YOU ARE MINE.'"
(ISAIAH 43:1)

Strength And Courage Through The Journey Of Cancer Treatment

Dear Heavenly Father,

We come to You today with hearts both heavy and hopeful. We pray for strength and courage for all those going through the journey of cancer treatment. Lord, You know the struggles, the weariness, the pain, and the moments of uncertainty they face. Surround them with Your peace that surpasses all understanding, filling their spirits with resilience and hope.

Guide the hands of their caregivers, doctors, and all who support them, granting wisdom and skill to bring about healing. When they feel weak, may they lean on You, finding a wellspring of strength they never knew they had. Remind them, Lord, that they are not alone. Let Your love shine brightly in their darkest moments, bringing comfort and the assurance of Your constant presence.

We pray for moments of rest, glimpses of joy, and faith to believe in the power of healing and transformation. May each step in this journey draw them closer to You, reminding them of their incredible strength, resilience, and the beauty of life.

In Your holy name, we pray. Amen.

A Prayer for Adult Children

Heavenly Father,

I lift my adult children into Your loving hands, entrusting them to Your guidance, protection, and provision. You know their hearts, their struggles, and the paths they walk. Lord, draw them closer to You and fill their lives with Your peace, joy, and purpose.

Give them wisdom to make decisions aligned with Your will. Surround them with friends and mentors who encourage their growth and inspire their faith. When they face challenges, remind them of Your unfailing presence and teach them to lean on You for strength and direction.

Father, I ask that You bless their relationships, work, and dreams. Protect them from harm and lead them away from anything that might steal their joy or peace. Help them to grow in character, resilience, and love, reflecting Your light to the world.

Lord, as their parent, grant me the grace to release them into Your care. May I trust You with their journey, knowing You love them more than I ever could. Thank You for the gift of being their parent and for Your eternal faithfulness in their lives.

In Jesus' name, Amen.

A Prayer for Women Battling Cancer

Heavenly Father,

We come to You with hearts full of compassion and hope, lifting up women who are courageously fighting cancer. You know each of their names, their struggles, and their fears. Lord, we ask for Your divine presence to surround them, offering comfort in moments of pain and peace amidst uncertainty.

Grant them the strength to endure the challenges of treatment and the grace to face each day with courage. Touch their bodies with Your healing hand, restoring health and vitality according to Your perfect will. Bless the doctors, nurses, and caregivers who support them, giving them wisdom and compassion.

Lord, be their refuge when they feel weary, and their light when the path seems dark. Fill their spirits with hope and remind them they are not alone—that You walk this journey with them. Surround them with love, from family, friends, and community, to uplift them in their time of need.

May they feel Your presence in every breath and trust in Your unending grace. In Jesus' name, we pray.

Amen.

A Prayer for Women Balancing Life's Responsibilities

Heavenly Father,

We come before You today, lifting up women who are striving to balance the many responsibilities placed upon them. Lord, You see their hearts, their strength, and their tireless efforts as they care for their families, dedicate themselves to work, and juggle countless other commitments.

Grant them Your peace, which surpasses all understanding, to calm the chaos and fill their spirits with rest. Remind them, Father, that they do not carry these burdens alone, for You are their refuge and strength, an ever-present help in their time of need.

Empower them with wisdom to prioritize what matters most and courage to release what is beyond their control. Pour into them a spirit of grace, that they may show compassion to themselves as much as they do to others. Surround them with a supportive community to share their load and uplift their hearts.

Lord, may they find joy even in the midst of challenges and lean on Your unchanging love as their ultimate source of hope and renewal. In Your name, we pray.

Amen.

A Prayer for the Strength to Forgive

Heavenly Father,

I come before You with a heart burdened by pain and memories that linger. You know the hurts I carry and the people who have caused them. Today, I lift them up to You, not with bitterness but with a desire for healing. Lord, I ask for Your strength, for I cannot forgive on my own. Teach me to release the chains of resentment that bind my soul, knowing that forgiveness is a gift You first extended to me.

Fill my heart with compassion and grace, even for those who have wronged me. Remind me that forgiveness is not about excusing actions but about freeing myself to walk in Your peace. May I trust Your justice and timing, laying down my need for revenge or understanding. Help me see those who hurt me through Your eyes, recognizing their own pain and struggles.

Father, as I pray for them, I also ask You to heal me. Restore what has been broken and replace anger with love. May my willingness to forgive reflect Your love and bring glory to Your name.

In Jesus' name, I pray. Amen.

WRITTEN BY:

Beverly Little, M.Ed
CERTIFIED TRANSFORMATION LIFE COACH

I am a certified Transformation Life Coach and founder of The Caffeinated Writer, LLC and Founder of Mindset & Soul Shifting Coaching. With certifications in Journal Therapy, Mindset Coaching, and Purposeful Life Coaching, I am dedicated to helping clients conquer obstacles and unlock their true potential.

My unique, supportive approach empowers individuals to find clarity, purpose, and personal growth, guiding them through the challenges they can't overcome alone, transforming mindsets, and shifting lives toward meaningful progress and fulfillment.

I am a published author, Podcast host, and avid photographer.

- (f) www.facebook.com/profile.php?id=61566144231484
- (f) https://www.facebook.com/groups/535146189210609
- (ig) @mindsetsoulshifting
- (🌐) mindsetsoulshifting.com

God Is Our Refuge

"THE NAME OF THE LORD IS A STRONG
TOWER; THE RIGHTEOUS MAN RUNS INTO IT
AND IS SAFE."
(PROVERBS 18:10)

Father Heal My Soul-Fracture

Father in the name of Jesus, I come to you laying my emotional wounds at your feet. I acknowledge and confess my hurt, disappointment, brokenness and even my struggle to heal. My heart is heavy, my mind is racing, I feel overwhelmed and weak in my soul. I am desperately seeking rest from this turmoil. Lord, please show me how to navigate through this soul-fracture.

By faith, I have confidence in Hebrews 4:15 For we do not have a high priest who is unable to sympathize with our weaknesses, but one who in every respect has been tempted as we are, yet without sin.

As I confess your word, I am reminded that I am not alone and that you sympathize with my emotional burdens. I choose to trust you in this storm, as I release any unforgiveness, resentment and even offense from every source of my pain.

Strengthen my heart and mind, fill me with your wisdom and courage, let your love and presence overtake me. Father, allow resilience to rise, grace to stabilize and balance me as I receive your restorative power, mercy and deliverance this day!

In Jesus name Amen

Father Heal My Broken Sight

Father in the name of Jesus, I come to you in need of my spiritual sight being restored. I ask that every blinded area of my life be penetrated by the power of your living word. Holy Spirit guide me beyond my natural sight as I realize I am not in alignment with Gods' will. This blindness is a result of my bad choices and my sin, and it has disrupted and distracted the wisdom and insight that you desire in my life. It has kept me bound from your promises and scattered my perceptions.

Lord, I repent for my sin and ask that you remove these scales of distraction and destruction! I desire to walk out of this darkness and have clarity for your purposes and your agenda for my life. According to your word in II Corinthians 3:16 But whenever anyone turns to the Lord, the veil is taken away. I trust your word and thank you in advance that the veil is removed and that I now have a renewed and refreshed spiritual sight through the lens of your word and your power in Jesus Name, Amen.

Father Heal My Trauma

Father in the name of Jesus, I come to you like the woman at the well in John 4. Indeed, I have a thirst that cannot be quenched with natural water. My soul is in a deficit that is causing more pain than words can express, and my life is full of sin that has tried to mask the trauma I've experienced. Many days I have appeared calm on the outside, but my inner child is screaming for help! Jesus you are the master therapist, and I come to you to heal my inner wounds.

I release this burden of trying to hide my trauma and I acknowledge that being totally honest and transparent with you is the start of breaking free from these cycles of destruction.

By faith I exchange my traumatic experiences for a true encounter with you just as that woman at the well did. I surrender to the release of your wisdom, guidance and strategy through counsel for my healing. I trust as I drink from this well which is your word, I will be strengthened and empowered on my journey to a full recovery in Jesus name Amen

Father Heal my Heart

Father in the name of Jesus, I place my heart in your hands. It has been broken by circumstances, bad decisions, self-inflicted sabotage and many other outside forces that have penetrated my love walk. I come asking you to forgive me for destructive behaviors and words that have come from a deceitful heart. I have operated in guilt, anger, jealousy, greed, fear, hostility, shame and even deception that has grieved the Holy Spirit.

Today I decide as I stand at the crossroads of my life, the crossroads of being honest with myself and honest with my God that I take accountability for these evil desires from my heart. I repent for the contamination I have allowed to flow from me that may have impacted others negatively as well and I ask for deliverance and breakthrough in this area of my life.

I trust your word according to Psalm 51:10, Father, create in me a clean heart and please renew a right spirit within me. Lord, turn my heart of stone into a heart of flesh. I desire to reflect and walk in love as my broken heart is mended in Jesus might and matchless name I pray, Amen.

Father Heal my Scattered Mind

Mighty God, thank you for giving me the power and authority to pull down every stronghold in my mind that tries to exalt itself above your word. Thank you for giving me the mind of Christ and the confidence that I am mentally well. My mind is coherent and prepared for this new day as I may face obstacles, levels of uncertainty and direct assaults from the enemy. I thank you that I pray from a vantage point of victory through Christ Jesus.

As I intently follow your instructions according to Ephesians 6:17 concerning taking up the helmet of salvation and the sword of the spirit, I am empowered as I fasten it on to function properly protecting my head. As my command center, I realize that my mind must be renewed daily by the word of God as I dominate and destroy opinions, worldviews, cultural standards and old mindsets that do not align with your standards.

Thank you, Lord, for healing my scattered mind and exchanging it for a focus on eternity, for future promises manifesting in my life and protection over my mental health that you purchased through your blood on the cross for me.

Amen

WRITTEN BY:

Dr. Orienthia Speakman, CPsyc.D

CEO, AUTHOR, TRANSFORMATIONAL COACH & LICENSED COUNSELOR

With over two decades of experience in ministerial leadership, Orienthia Speakman is a strategic optimist with an undeniable resilience that has impacted woman globally.

Her ability to integrate scripture and psychology has empowered individuals towards wholeness.

Through her work as an Author, Transformational Coach and Licensed Counselor, her focus on personal growth and healing enables women to overcome difficulties such as divorce and trauma, transforming them into resilient individuals who actively pursue their divine purpose.

Serving as CEO and Founder of Speak O Worldwide, this mentorship hub and platform provides spiritual and soul-care for those who are brokenhearted through her books, seminars, and workshops. Collaborations and engagement with other leaders through this transition is close to her heart. She strongly believes in bridging the gap between unwanted realities to desired results.

Orienthia and her husband Vincent along with their blended family of five reside in Stone Mountain, GA.

- Orienthia Speakman
- @drospeaks
- www.orienthiaspeakman.com

God Is Our Deliverer

"THE RIGHTEOUS CRY OUT, AND THE LORD HEARS THEM; HE DELIVERS THEM FROM ALL THEIR TROUBLES."
(PSALM 34:17)

Divine Healing and Restoration: A Prayer for Inner Peace and Health

Dear Heavenly Father,

I come before You with an open and humble heart, seeking Your healing touch upon my body, mind, and spirit.

Father, in Your infinite wisdom and love, please guide me through this journey to health and wholeness in You. Please renew within me a deep sense of peace, washing away my fears, my doubts, and my weariness. May Your strength flow through every cell in my body, restoring vitality, energy, and resilience.

Lord, please grant me your patience to trust in Your timing and courage to face each new day with hope and surround me with Your light, filling my heart with calmness, my mind with clarity, and my spirit with unwavering faith.

Amen.

Building Your Confidence in the Lord

Dear Heavenly Father,

I come before You today, seeking to build my confidence in You. Lord, I confess that I often struggle with self-doubt and fear. But I know that You are my Rock, my Refuge, and my Redeemer.

I pray that You would help me to trust in Your goodness, Your love, and Your sovereignty. Give me the confidence to know that You are always with me, guiding me, and empowering me to overcome any obstacle.

Help me to remember that my identity and worth come from You, and that I am loved, valued, and cherished by You. Build my confidence in You, Lord, that I may walk in faith, hope, and courage.

In Jesus' name, I pray. Amen.

Trust in the Lord

Dear Heavenly Father,

I come before You today, seeking to trust in You with all my heart. Lord, I confess that I often struggle with doubt and fear. But I know that You are faithful, trustworthy, and true.

I pray that You would help me to trust in Your goodness, Your love, and Your sovereignty. Give me the faith to believe that You are always working for my good, even when I don't understand. Help me to trust in Your timing, Your wisdom, and Your power.

May I rest in Your presence, knowing that You are my Rock, my Refuge, and my Redeemer. I trust in You, Lord, with all my heart.

In Jesus' name, I pray. Amen.

Seeking God for His Guidance

Dear Heavenly Father,

I come before You today, seeking Your guidance in my life. Lord, I confess that I often feel uncertain and unsure about the path ahead. But I know that You are the all-knowing, all-wise, and all-loving God who desires to lead me in the way I should go.

I pray that You would grant me wisdom, discernment, and clarity of mind as I seek to follow Your will. Guide me in my decisions, Lord, and help me to trust in Your sovereignty.

May Your Spirit lead me, comfort me, and empower me to walk in obedience to Your Word. I seek Your guidance, Lord, and trust that You will direct my paths.

In Jesus' name, I pray. Amen.

Seeking Wisdom from God

Dear Heavenly Father,

I come before You today, seeking wisdom from above. Lord, I confess that I often rely on my own understanding and limited knowledge. But I know that Your wisdom is infinite, and that You desire to give me wisdom generously.

I pray that You would grant me wisdom to navigate the complexities of life, to make decisions that honor You, and to discern Your will. Give me wisdom to speak words that are gracious and truthful, and to act in ways that are just and compassionate.

May Your wisdom guide me, Lord, and may I trust in Your goodness and sovereignty.

I ask for wisdom in Jesus' name. Amen.

WRITTEN BY:

Coach Allison G. Daniels

PASTOR, BOOK WRITING COACH AND AUTHOR

Coach Allison G. Daniels, is a native of Washington, D. C. She holds a bachelor's degree in business administration from Strayer University.

She is an International Awarding-Winning, 27 X Bestselling Author who has written over 45 plus books, Co-Author of 27 books, Multi-Visionary Author of the Book Series "Empowered to Win", Unshakable Faith, Women Be Free and Women Empowered to Lead. She is a multi-visionary and master collaborator strategist for non-fiction authors in Christian-fiction, non-fiction and children's books. She is the recipient of the Presidential Lifetime Achievement Award. She retired after a 38-year career with the Federal Government. She is a Pastor, wife of 23 years to her husband Earl, mother of two beautiful queens, Damona, Kristian and grandmother of one grandson Grayson.

Coach Allison G. Daniels is an International Diversity Trainer for Women's Issues. She received her license in October 2014 to Preach the Gospel. In 2019 during the pandemic God placed it on her heart to launch AGD Publishing Services, LLC, which is a publishing and consulting company where we offer Coaching, Consulting, and Independent Publishing Services. She is the creator of the "30 Day Write to Finish Book Writing Program and Empowerment Academy for Writer, "a mastermind group focused on teaching the strategies of leveraging books to build a business with multiple income streams.

She has been featured on ABC, Radio One, WBGR, Black Enterprise, Good Morning Washington, The Washington Informer, and numerous other media outlets. Her journey to impact women and fulfil her life's purpose has led her to grace the cover of her own magazine: Empowered to Win, Global Christian Magazine as well as Nspire Christian Magazine, K.I.SH. Magazine, Tap-In Magazine and GLEMB Magazine (Nigeria) Top Leader and featured on various billboards. She has been featured in over 300 news articles worldwide, including Voyage ATL. She has been recognized as one of the Top 50 Courageous Women in Business, Leadership and Entertainment, as well as Hoinser Top 50 Entrepreneurs. Her personal philosophy is: "There is power in sharing your story and speaking your truth because your #Story Matters!" WRITE IT NOW!

God Is Our Teacher

"I WILL INSTRUCT YOU AND TEACH YOU IN
THE WAY YOU SHOULD GO; I WILL COUNSEL
YOU WITH MY LOVING EYE ON YOU."
(PSALM 32:8)

The Rock Higher Than I (Psalm 61)

Father God Daddy God I thank You that You are The Rock higher than I. The pain of Fibromyalgia has overwhelmed me. I know Your word say You are the God that heals. I cry out to You today and lay it all down to You to receive the healing I need from this pain that affects every fiber of my being.

Your word says to trust You with my whole heart and not lean to my own understanding so today I cast all my care frustration disappointment overwhelming fear and anguish of this pain that has wracked my body mind and spirit onto You. I trust and believe Jesus was wounded for my transgressions bruised for my iniquities the chastisement of my peace was upon and with His stripes I am healed today. You heal the broken hearted binding up their wounds. I receive the word to every cell tissue organ and organ system of my body to heal me of every manner of sickness and disease.

I thank You that You watch over Your word and hasten to perform. I thank You for all Your benefits: forgiveness of sins redeems my life from destruction crowns me with lovingkindness and tender mercies satisfies my mouth with good things so that my youth is renewed as the eagle's. I thank You because You set Your love upon me and deliver me with long life you satisfy me and show me Your salvation and when my heart is overwhelmed You lead me to the rock that's higher than I.

For this I give You praise glory honor Majesty You so rightly deserve.

The God of All Comfort

F ather God I thank You that Your word says You are the God of all comfort. You comfort us that we may comfort others in any trouble with the comfort we ourselves receive from You.

This season sometimes weighs heavily on me because of the loved ones lost. My heart is overwhelmed as it begins with remembrance of the loss of my brother, my namesake. I know that Jesus is the reason for every season and I'm thankful and grateful for Your love toward us in giving Him to die for our sins. I thank You also that You heal the broken hearted binding up their wounds and You are near to them.

Be near me now I pray. that I pass through rejoicing even as I remember the relationship my brother Karl and I have and I sorrow not as those that don't have hope in the resurrection and focus on the good times we had the fun how he looked out for me took me shopping showered me with love and sold me my first car.

Lord so many good memories that far outweigh bad ones. I thank You Lord that You always cause me to triumph in Christ Jesus and I am more than a conqueror in Jesus. I choose Your joy which is my strength to press through look to the hills knowing all my help comes from You. Thank You Lord for being the God of all comfort.

I receive it in Jesus name that my heart be not troubled or afraid but have joy unspeakable and full of glory and peace that passes all understanding to keep my heart and mind through Christ Jesus.

The Rock Higher Than I

Hear my cry oh God attend unto my prayer from the ends of the earth will I cry unto Thee and when my heart is overwhelmed lead me to the Rock that's higher than I.

This is a new road Lord and I don't know how to travel it alone. You said You would never leave or forsake me. I need to know and experience that like never before. I thank You for the scripture eto know there is a place higher than the situation I now face that You are the rock higher than the lowliness I feel right now. That Your name is a strong the righteous can run into and be safe.

I thank You and praise You for that place of safety now as I feel alone and afraid. I'm in Your safety. I've prayed I would never see a day like this one yet here I am and know that nothing catches You by surprise and nothing happens to me that You don't already know but it's for a reason and a season and too shall pass. Your word says many are the afflictions of the righteous but You Lord deliver out of them all.

Thank You Lord for deliverance. Thank You Lord You are the Rock higher than I. I will lift up mine eyes to youth author and finisher of my faith. You will not assuredly nor leave me without aid or support.

I trust You Lord with my whole heart and not leant to what I understand. Thank You for being the Rock of my salvation the God that saves heals and delivers.

Daddy God

Father God Daddy God there are many things that trouble me nowadays I know that Your word says to cast all my cares on You for You care for me. Its just that sometimes they seem so heavy as I cast them they fall back with me and I take them back. Your word says Your yoke is easy and Your burden is light. I have trouble releasing everything to Your care.

I thank You for Holy Spirit who is a helper a comforter to lead and guide me into all truth and show me things to come and Minister to me, Jesus. You've shown me time and time again that You are good and good all the time.

Help me Lord I pray in Jesus' name realize this time that if You did it before You'll do it again because Your Words says You're the same God yesterday today and forever. Father God with my whole heart I confess that I trust You and not lean to what I understand but in all my ways. I acknowledge You that You direct my path. You order my steps. You lead and guide me through this season that I faint not but believe to see Your goodness in the land of the living. That I trust You to be a shield for me the glory and lifter up of my head above my enemies round about.

I thank You that You will see me safely through. Thank You for Your loving kindness tender mercies grace and truth in Your word that You watch over and had to perform on my behalf.

Lord You Are The Strength of My Heart

Father I stretch my hands to Thee no other help I know. If Thou withdraw Thyself from me whether shall I go? Who have I in heaven but Thee and there is none upon earth that I desire besides Thee.

Lord, You are the strength of my heart and my portion forever. I trust You, Lord. You are my help and strength a very present help in trouble. You've not given me a spirit of fear but a spirit of power love and a sound mind.

Help me to activate it in times like these so that I rise above all the enemy sends as an attack against me. So that with my full armor on and my shield of faith I can quench every fiery dark of the devil and stand fast in the liberty where Christ has set me free.

I want to have confidence like the Hebrew boys that You are well able to deliver me from anything as I'm obedient to do Your will. When the enemy comes against me like a flood You raise a standard against them and I have a way to escape.

Thank You Lord that Your Grace is sufficient and Your strength is made perfect in weakness that when I'm weak I can say I'm strong in You and the power of Your might. No weapon formed against me shall prosper. I shall prosper and be in good health even as my soul prospers. Thank You Lord.

WRITTEN BY:

Minister Carlette Long Boyd

MINISTER, GRANDMOTHER AND MOTHER

Mother of 4 children 2 guys 2 young ladies grandmother of 7 beautiful granddaughters listened Minister active in Leadership at Saints Tabernacle Church of The Lord Jesus Christ Sunday School teacher for Adult and Eagles Nest (children) director of SALT-TAG women's ministry at church program director for church plays have one chapter of book published on Amazon. Prophetic scribe write poetry inspirational verses and inspired song under Peace Speaker Ministries LPN

(f) PEACE Speaker Ministries

God Is Faithful to His Promises

"THE LORD IS FAITHFUL TO ALL HIS
PROMISES AND LOVING TOWARD ALL HE HAS
MADE."
(PSALM 145:13)

Thee Answer

It isn't money.
It's not your race, sex or if you buy or borrow.
It's not the size of your home, or the labels you wear.
Things are here today and gone tomorrow.

It's not your social status or
the letters behind your name.
It's not your looks, number of friends,
your age or fame

People come and go.
It's not the size of your bank account,
places you've been or how much you know.

It is caring, and compassion for your fellow man,
to help and serve as much as you can.
Its hope and faith in the Lord above.

The answer my dear friend is-
Love

Last Year

There were events that caused shock and awe.
You couldn't believe the things you heard and saw
But, you made it
Remember the time when your life could have ended?
Yet here you stand healthy and mended.
You made it
Some people who celebrated with you before
Have made their transition and are here no more
But, you made it
Even those times when life was rough
And you felt you had enough
You made it
Now that you've been given a brand new year
Make it your best,
There's a reason why you're still here.
Let go of the anger.
Choose to love instead.
Find your purpose and move ahead.
Choose happiness instead of sorrow
For you're not promised to see tomorrow.
Strive for greatness and never quit
Because by the grace of God
You made it!

Good morning, Joy!

Good morning joy
Farewell pain
Today I'm prepared for victory
To shimmy in the rain
To find a blessing in every moment
The past does not matter
To discover blooms amongst the weeds
And hear a bird's song above the chatter
To seize the gift of a brand new day
For I am too blessed for stress
I'll adorn my garment of praise
For today I choose happiness.

Really God?

You want me to forgive who?
How can this be?
How can I forgive them after all
the hurtful things they said to me?

Really God?
You want me to be kind?
You know the horrible things they did
almost made me lose my mind

Really God?
You want me to leave everything in your hands-
humble myself and
make moves I don't understand?

Really God?
Is this up for debate?
You want me to show them love
when all they do is hate?

Really God?
I'll do what you tell me to do and
I'll keep my mind on you

If my blessing takes time to receive
I'll have faith and believe

I'll keep my head to the sky
For you are not a man that you should lie

God, I'll keep my mind on you
Whatever you tell me to do, I'll do

The Storm

The rain keeps on falling.
You said you would be my guide.
I thought about giving up but your arms are open wide.

Lord I'm weak and I need your hand.
Lift me up so that I can stand.

Be a shield around me and protect me from this storm.
When the cold wind of life surrounds me, Lord please keep me warm.

The thunder is so fierce and the lightening frightens me
The hail is beating hard and the sun I cannot see.

I'm stepping out on faith as bird learning to fly.
Lord, I know you're watching from your home on high.

Even though I don't understand the trials I'm going through,
I will not complain and completely lean on you.

I surrender everything my soul and my hearts desire.
I will not doubt you Savior the devil is a liar.

I lift my hands to you Lord.
Send you're anointing today.
And give me a brand new spirit in Jesus name I pray.

WRITTEN BY:

Nedra V. Ware

POET, AUTHOR, REGISTERED NURSE, MOTHER AND WIFE

Hi, I'm Nedra V. Ware, a wife, mother, and registered nurse with a passion for writing. Over the years, I've published two collections of poetry (The Sweetest Sound) (There's Something About September) and a children's book (Dette's Mountain) , each designed to inspire, encourage, and uplift.

Whether I'm at home with my family or working in healthcare, I believe in the power of words to heal and motivate. Writing allows me to share hope, laughter, and positivity with others.

 ardensenihpoetry.net

God Is Holy

"HOLY, HOLY, HOLY IS THE LORD OF HOSTS;
THE WHOLE EARTH IS FULL OF HIS GLORY!"
(ISAIAH 6:3)

Poetic Healing

Many ancient Christian writers penned poetry to express their faith and intimacy with God. I can relate. I delight in rhyming with God in prayer—creatively communicating with my Creator and Master Innovator.

Let us poetically pray:

> Beloved Jehovah Rapha
> Healer of all
> On Your Love, we depend
> On Your Name, we call
>
> In You, we delight
> Basking in Your sight
> Clinging to You
> With all our might
>
> In our weakness
> Is Your Strength
> Which carries us
> Through any length
>
> Isaiah 40:29 says,
> "He gives strength to the weary and increases the power of the weak."
> Therefore, it is You, Lord
> We must seek
>
> James 5:15 says,
> "And the prayer offered in faith will make the sick person well;"
> May we stay close to You
> And this we'll be able to tell
>
> Jeremiah 17:14 says,
> "Heal me, Lord, and I will be healed; save me, and I will be saved,"
> May this be our prayer
> On many days
>
> Prayers for healing and comfort
> Peace and love
> May we seek You, God
> Like a trusting dove
>
> Your Name of all names
> Held on high
> We trust in Your healing
> And with our faith, we 'fly!'
>
> In Jesus' Healing Name, Amen.

Savoring Liminal Spaces

How do you wait in liminal spaces, the in-between space—the threshold—of what was and what will be? Do you wait calmly or anxiously?

In November 2024, I participated in a 5-day "Biblical Liminal Spaces Challenge" by LiveLiving.org.

During that time, I wrote a version of this poetic prayer:

> Dear Patient God,
>
> Please help us savor time in liminal space
> As there's much to take in during the wait
> Anchor us to enjoy what You have created on Earth
> Elements that have been in front of us since our birth
>
> The smell of flowers
> The sight of trees
> The buzzing of bumble bees
> The feeling of the wind in our hair
> Help us pause and take in the sounds of nature we hear
>
> And may we not forget... The beautiful sunrise and sunset.
>
> May the wait within liminal space
> Be filled with Your grace
> And increased faith

As You fill our plates
Like a sacred date—with You!

No doubt, that we can
Eliminate the fuss
That we tend to stir up
In the liminal spaces around us

Please increase our patience
As you set us free
Reminding us that our liminal spaces
Will not be for eternity.

Amen.

Your Presence

"Let us come into His presence with thanksgiving..."
Psalm 95:2

Today is National Day of Prayer, but coming into the Presence of God and praying, daily, is the key to spiritual intimacy with our Creator. While visiting New York last December, I was led to write "Your Presence" in my cozy hotel room during my morning devotional time. I shared it with The Unsealed community online and am blessed to share it with you, too. I hope it inspires you to bask in God's Presence—and pray each day.

Dear Ever-Present God,

Your Presence is what I seek
Your Presence is where we meet
Your Presence brings me peace
Your Presence is for the bold and meek

Your Presence is unmatched
Your Presence is the latch
Your Presence I respect
Your Presence is where we connect

Your Presence is golden
Your Presence is emboldening
Your Presence beautifully mends
Your Presence is a gem

Your Presence is dependable
Your Presence is commendable
Your Presence is my truth
Your Presence is my root

Your Presence holds my hand
Your Presence is time with my Best Friend
Your Presence has no end
Your Presence is where I stand!

In Jesus' Name, Amen.

Comfort During Grief

Navigating grief is certainly not limited to one day, but coming up on August 30 is National Grief Awareness Day, a day dedicated to grief awareness, support, and education. May this prayer help comfort those in need.

Dear Comforting God,

I pray for Your children who are grieving
May they never stop believing
That You are by their side
During this heartbreaking ride.

Please help them, Lord
To keep their trust in You
Comfort them
And show them what to do.

Ease their pain during this 'rain'
As "You are close to the brokenhearted
And save the crushed in spirit." (Psalm 34:18)
Please remind them of this, Lord Let them hear it.

Matthew 5:4 highlights this some more
If need be, may they print this verse
And hang it on their door:
"God blesses those who mourn,
For they will be comforted."

May they affirm,
"I can do all things through Christ
Who strengthens me." (Philippians 4:13)
Touch them, Lord, and let them see.

In Jesus' Name, may this be!
Amen.

Healing from Fear

In honor of National Live Fearless Day today, I share this poetic prayer. The late Nikki Giovanni inspired it. I challenged myself to read the original version at an Open Mic Night hosted by The Unsealed.

Dear Fearless God,

FEAR
Why is it everywhere
When You have not given us a spirit of fear
But rather of "power, love, and a sound mind" (2 Timothy 1:7)
Why do we let fear move us from You, The Divine?

Instead of fear gripping us
Lord, please help us to trust
And take fear by its head
And put it to bed

May we let it fall
Even squish it against a wall
Letting it flop, drop
And stop!

According to Nikki Giovanni, "Fear should be a spice"
That would be nice
As long as we don't let it become like ice
Causing us to lose the heat of our internal God-given device

May we keep fear in its right place
And not let it waste
What You have waiting for us with grace
And what we're here to taste

As Psalm 34:8 says,
"Taste and see that the Lord is good;"
Please help us move through fear
The way we should!

Amen.

WRITTEN BY:

Penny A. Powell

FREELANCE WRITER, AUTHOR, CHRIST-CENTERED
STRETCHING INSTRUCTOR

Born and raised on the beautiful island of Bermuda, Penny Powell is a freelance writer living in Fleming Island, Florida. She has a master's degree in humanities with a concentration in journalism and is the author of "Rhyming with God: Poetic Prayers and Reflections," which will be published by Wipf and Stock Publishers in 2025.

Penny is a contributor at ChristianDevotions.us and contributed to Judson Press' Summer 2024 issue of "The Secret Place." Along with her passion for devotional writing, Penny enjoys teaching a Christ-centered class—Stretch, Strengthen, and Relax—in her community.

(f) penny.powell.79

God Is Unchanging

"JESUS CHRIST IS THE SAME YESTERDAY AND
TODAY AND FOREVER."
(HEBREWS 13:8)

A Prayer of Gratitude for Life and Guidance

Loving God,

Thank You for the precious gift of life, for each new day filled with opportunities to love, grow, and serve. Even when trials come my way, I know You walk with me, strengthening my spirit and filling my heart with hope.

I am deeply grateful for the guidance of Your beloved saints. Thank You, Mother Teresa, for your unwavering example of compassion and humility, reminding me to see Your face in others. Thank You, Sto. Niño, for the gift of joy and faith, helping me to trust in Your promises. Thank You, Mama Mary, for your loving care and intercession, always leading me closer to Your Son, Jesus.

Lord, I praise You for the health and strength You have given me, a constant reminder of Your goodness. Even in life's struggles, I am sustained by Your grace and lifted by Your love. You turn every challenge into an opportunity for growth and every moment of doubt into a chance to deepen my faith.

A Prayer for Work and Business Success

Heavenly Father,

I come to You with a grateful heart for the work and opportunities You have entrusted to me. Thank You for the skills, talents, and wisdom You have blessed me with, which allow me to provide for myself and my family. Lord, I place my job and business into Your hands, knowing that with You, all things are possible.

Grant me the strength to overcome challenges and the patience to endure setbacks. Help me to always act with integrity, humility, and excellence, so that my work reflects Your goodness and brings honor to Your name. Guide me to make wise decisions that align with Your purpose and lead to growth and prosperity.

Bless my efforts, Lord, that they may bear fruit—not only for my success but also for the benefit of others. May my work serve as a channel of Your blessings, helping me to uplift those around me and contribute positively to the world.

In moments of doubt or difficulty, remind me of Your constant presence and unfailing love. Teach me to trust in Your plan, knowing that You are with me every step of the way. Give me the courage to embrace new opportunities, the wisdom to learn from my experiences, and the vision to see Your hand at work in all that I do.

Thank You, Lord, for providing me with a healthy life, a hopeful heart, and the ability to create and grow. May You continue to guide my path, bless my efforts, and use my work to fulfill Your greater plan for my life. In Jesus' name, I pray. Amen.

A Prayer for Healing

Loving Father,

I come before You with a heart full of faith, asking for Your divine healing. You are the ultimate healer, Lord, and I trust in Your power to restore my body, mind, and spirit. I surrender my pain, my fears, and my worries to You, knowing You care deeply for me.

Through the intercession of Mother Teresa, who dedicated her life to serving others with love and faith, I pray for her guidance and blessings. May her prayers touch my life and bring me comfort and strength during this time of healing.

I also call upon Sto. Niño, the source of hope and miracles. Dear Sto. Niño, with childlike faith, I ask for Your healing grace to remove every sickness, especially the cyst in my body. Renew my health and restore my strength so that I may continue to serve and glorify God in all that I do.

Lord, fill me with Your peace, calm my fears, and replace my worries with trust in Your perfect plan. Surround me with love and support from my family and friends, and guide the hands of those who care for me. Let every moment of this journey draw me closer to You, deepening my faith and reliance on Your mercy.

Thank You, Lord, for Your healing touch, for the intercession of Your saints, and for the hope You give me each day. I claim the healing You have promised, and I praise You for the restoration that is already on its way.

In Jesus' name, I pray. Amen.

A Prayer for Success in 2025

Heavenly Father,

As I prepare to enter 2025, I come before You with a heart full of hope and faith. Thank You for the blessings of the past year—the lessons learned, the opportunities given, and the challenges that have made me stronger. I entrust this new year to You, Lord, knowing that Your plans are always for my good.

Bless the work of my hands, Lord, and guide my every step toward success. Help me to set meaningful goals and give me the discipline and wisdom to achieve them. May my efforts bear fruit that brings not only personal fulfillment but also serves others and glorifies Your name. Grant me clarity in my decisions, courage in pursuing new opportunities, and resilience in facing any obstacles. Surround me with supportive people who inspire and uplift me, and help me to be a source of encouragement to those I meet.

I ask for Your protection over my job, business, and all that I do. Multiply the resources You've entrusted to me and open doors that no one can close. Through the intercession of Mother Teresa and Sto. Niño, I seek their prayers and guidance to stay focused, humble, and grounded in faith as I work toward my goals.

Lord, let this year be a time of growth, success, and abundance—not just in material blessings, but in love, joy, and peace. Help me to remain grateful in all circumstances and to trust in Your perfect timing. With You, Lord, I know that 2025 will be a year of triumph, and I will praise You for every blessing that comes my way. In Jesus' name, I pray. Amen.

WRITTEN BY:

Kimberly Mae Culasing

HR PROFESSIONAL AND SOCIAL MEDIA MANAGER

With nearly 5 years of experience as an HR professional and 4 years as a dedicated freelancer, I bring expertise and adaptability to every role I take. As the eldest and breadwinner of my family, I am driven by responsibility, resilience, and a passion for growth.

 www.facebook.com/kimberlymae.culasing

Finding My Way Back

Lord, I come to You right now in the name of Your Son, Jesus, and I thank You for this day. I thank You for blessing, protecting and keeping me Lord, for watching over me as I slept. Thank You for never leaving me nor forsaking me. I ask that You strengthen me right now Lord, and keep me as I walk through this hard season of my life. Let me feel Your presence in a tangible way as I find my way back to Your light from the darkness that sought to overtake me.

Bless me Lord, mentally, physically, spiritually, emotionally, and financially. Give me boldness to live the life You purposed for me. Order my steps and send laborers to my fields to help me fulfill the calling on my life. I thank You now for every good and perfect gift coming to me, and that I will see the goodness of the Lord in the land of the living. Right now, I give You all the honor, glory and praise for these and all other blessings You have set before me and for loving me like You do.

In Jesus Name I pray, Amen.

WRITTEN BY:

Regina Sunshine Robinson

AUTHOR, COACH, PUBLISHER, EMPOWERMENT SPECIALIST

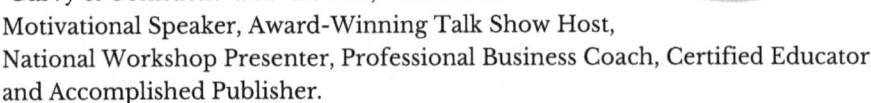

Regina Sunshine Robinson is an Empowerment Specialist and the CEO of Regina Sunshine Global Network. She is the author of two books, contributor to Chicken Soup for the Soul's "Curvy & Confident" and "Be You," Acclaimed Motivational Speaker, Award-Winning Talk Show Host, National Workshop Presenter, Professional Business Coach, Certified Educator, and Accomplished Publisher.

Regina's motto is "It's not over til I win," and she wins when she sees others WINNING!"

- (f) ReginaSunshineRobinson
- (ig) @regina_sunshine and @rsgntv
- (in) www.linkedin.com/in/regina-sunshine-robinson-064abb72
- (d) @reginasunshinerob
- (▶) @reginasunshineglobalnetwork

God Is the Giver of Good Gifts

"EVERY GOOD AND PERFECT GIFT IS FROM ABOVE, COMING DOWN FROM THE FATHER OF LIGHTS."
(JAMES 1:17)

A Prayer of Gratitude for Small Joys

Heavenly Father,

We come before You with hearts full of gratitude, for Your Word reminds us in 1 Thessalonians 5:18: "In every thing give thanks: for this is the will of God in Christ Jesus concerning you." Lord, we thank You for the small joys that fill our daily lives, often unnoticed yet brimming with Your presence.

Thank You for the warmth of sunlight on our faces, the gentle rustle of leaves in the breeze, and the laughter of a child. These moments, though fleeting, are reflections of Your abundant love and faithfulness. May we never overlook the beauty of a simple smile, the comfort of a kind word, or the satisfaction of work well done.

Teach us, Lord, to slow down and see Your hand in the little blessings—a cup of coffee shared with a friend, the vibrant colors of a sunrise, or the serenity of a quiet evening. Open our eyes to these gifts and let them fill our souls with joy and contentment.

Help us to live with hearts that sing Your praises, cherishing each moment as an opportunity to draw closer to You. Thank You for being the Giver of every good and perfect gift.

In Jesus' name, we pray.
Amen.

A Prayer for Strengthening Bonds and Nurturing Love

Heavenly Father,

We thank You for the gift of relationships, for the family and friends You have placed in our lives. Your Word in Colossians 3:14 reminds us, "And above all these things put on charity, which is the bond of perfectness." Lord, we ask for Your guidance to strengthen the bonds we share and nurture love that reflects Your grace.

Teach us patience and understanding when challenges arise, and help us to forgive one another as You have forgiven us. Fill our hearts with compassion, that we may support and uplift each other in times of need. Grant us the humility to listen, the wisdom to speak words of kindness, and the courage to build bridges where there are divides.

Lord, bless our families and friendships with joy and peace. May our homes be havens of love and faith, where Your presence is felt in every interaction. Help us to cherish the moments we share and to prioritize these relationships, cultivating a love that endures.

May we be instruments of Your love, building unity and bringing hope to those we hold dear. Thank You for Your example of perfect love that inspires us to love others deeply.

In Jesus' name, we pray. Amen.

A Prayer for Wisdom in Decision-Making

Heavenly Father,

We come before You, seeking Your divine guidance and wisdom in the decisions we face. Your Word in James 1:5 assures us, "If any of you lacks wisdom, you should ask God, who gives generously to all without finding fault, and it will be given to you." Lord, we stand on this promise, trusting in Your infinite understanding and loving counsel.

Grant us discernment to know what is right, courage to follow Your will, and patience to wait for Your perfect timing. Help us to lay aside our fears and doubts, leaning not on our own understanding but trusting fully in You. May our choices reflect Your truth and glorify Your name.

Lord, shield us from confusion and distractions. Help us to seek Your Word for clarity and to listen attentively to the whisper of Your Spirit. Guide our hearts to align with Yours, that we may pursue paths that bring peace, purpose, and blessings to ourselves and others.

Thank You for being our ever-present source of wisdom and strength. As we navigate life's uncertainties, we surrender all our plans to You, knowing that Your plans are good and perfect.

In Jesus' name, we pray. Amen.

A Prayer for Hope in Physical, Mental, and Spiritual Wellness

Heavenly Father,

We come to You with hearts seeking hope and healing, for Your Word in Jeremiah 30:17 promises, "But I will restore you to health and heal your wounds, declares the Lord." Thank You for being our Great Physician, the One who renews our bodies, minds, and spirits.

For those struggling with physical ailments, we ask for Your healing touch. Strengthen their bodies and grant them endurance as they walk this journey. May they feel Your presence, bringing comfort and peace amidst the challenges.

For those burdened with mental struggles, anxiety, or despair, we pray for clarity and calm. Uplift their spirits, remind them of their worth, and surround them with love and support. Replace fear with courage, and sorrow with joy.

For our spiritual wellness, Lord, draw us closer to You. Restore our souls and renew our faith. Help us to trust Your promises and to find strength in prayer and Scripture. Guide us to be vessels of Your hope, spreading light to others in their darkness.

Thank You, Lord, for the hope we find in You, a hope that never fades. We trust in Your power to make us whole.

In Jesus' name, we pray. Amen.

WRITTEN BY:

Crissa Lee Arcillas

SEO & SOCIAL MEDIA MARKETING EXPERT AND VIRTUAL ASSISTANT

Crissa Lee Arcillas is a dedicated mother and seasoned virtual assistant with over 13 years of experience. She excels in diverse roles, including administrative support, project management, SEO, and social media marketing. Currently working part-time, Crissa seamlessly balances her professional expertise with her personal life.

A devout Christian, she draws strength from her faith to guide her both in her work and daily life.

Crissa is passionate about helping businesses grow through her versatile skills and is committed to delivering excellence in every task she undertakes.

Christmas Prayer for Families with Loved Ones Abroad

Dear God,

This Christmas, our hearts are filled with both joy and longing. We're grateful for the love and sacrifices of our family, especially for those who are far away, working hard to support us. It's not easy to celebrate without them here, but we hold onto the love that connects us, no matter the miles between us.

We ask that You watch over them, Lord. Keep them safe, healthy, and surrounded by Your peace. Let them feel how much they are loved and missed during this special season. Give them strength when they feel alone and hope when the days feel hard.

For us here at home, help us to cherish the moments we have together and to honor the sacrifices being made for our family. May this Christmas remind us all of the power of love, the importance of family, and the promise that brighter days are ahead.

Thank You for the gift of Your Son, who teaches us to love selflessly and hold onto hope. Until we're reunited, please keep our hearts close and our spirits strong.

Amen.

WRITTEN BY:

Krisna Cuabo
SPECIAL EDUCATION TEACHER, ORDAINED PASTOR

Dr. Shannon Hall has been married for 15 years. She has 2 children and was born and raised in Orlando, Florida. The family now resides in Atlanta, Georgia, where Dr. Shannon Hall currently works for Dekalb County School as a Pre-K Special Education Teacher. Dr. Shannon Hall was called to the ministry in 1990.

In 1992, she joined Holy Tabernacles Church of Deliverance under Lewis I. Nicholson Senior, where she accepted her calling. It was there that she met her spiritual mother, Elder Elaine Lewis, who introduced her to Pastor Rosie E. Bess. Dr. Hall then served as an evangelist under her tutelage at the Independent Church of God, where she served until 2001. Dr. Hall transitioned to Georgia under God's guidance and instruction, where she participated in various ministries. She was ordained as a pastor while serving under Apostles Barbra and Leon Beeler. Additionally, Dr. Hall was part of the ministerial staff of Wings of Faith Ministries under the tutelage of Bishop Dreyfus Smith. She also served as an oversight pastor at Kingdom Living Ministries.

The scripture given to her by God was Romans 5:5:
"Now hope does not disappoint, because the love of God has been poured out in our hearts by the Holy Spirit who was given to us." Also Luke 4:18:
"The Spirit of the Lord is upon me, because he hath anointed me to preach the gospel to the poor; he hath sent me to heal the brokenhearted, to preach deliverance to the captives, and recovering of sight to the blind, to set at liberty them that are bruised."

In 2018 she founded "Women Walking Victoriously." On May 2021, Dr. Hall was affirmed as an apostle by Apostle Renaldo Turner in South Carolina and reaffirmed by Apostle Groves by the laying of hands and pouring of oil on June 4, 2022. Now she is currently a part of (KRIM) Kingdom Remnant International Ministries, where the presiding prelate is Apostle Alee Groves, and where she went through her consecration and anointing. Dr. Shannon Hall has accomplished great work.

God Is Our Light

"THE LORD IS MY LIGHT AND MY SALVATION;
WHOM SHALL I FEAR? THE LORD IS THE
STRONGHOLD OF MY LIFE; OF WHOM SHALL I
BE AFRAID?"
(PSALM 27:1)

Prayer for Mindfulness and a Renewed Mindset

Dear Heavenly Father, I humbly come before You to thank You for this day. I'm so grateful You allowed me to see this day, and I ask that Your will, not mine, be done. As I go through this day, please help me see, recognize, and speak Your blessings upon me and others in the area of mindfulness and mindset.

Lord, You have given me a sound mind, and I pray that You guide my thoughts and emotions to align with Your truth. Help me to release worries and burdens into Your capable hands and embrace the peace that surpasses all understanding. Keep me focused on what is good, pure, and worthy of praise, and give me the strength to turn away from negativity or self-doubt.

I also pray for those who are struggling with mental and emotional battles. Be their comfort and guide, just as You are for me. Help me to offer encouragement and kindness to others who may need to see Your light. May my words and actions reflect Your grace and bring hope to those around me.

Dear Lord, I ask for forgiveness for my shortcomings today. Bless my friends and family, those I talk to and those I don't, and be with all those who need You—whether they call on You or not. Lord, thank You for showing me Your Grace, Love, Mercy, and Generosity. Help me to always show the light of You to everyone I meet and encounter so that they know that what I do is not of me but You working through me.

In the name of Your Holy Mighty Son Jesus,
Amen.

Prayer for Restful Sleep and Peaceful Nights

Dear Lord, I humbly come before You to thank You for this day. I'm glad I had this day, and I ask that You help me make it through tomorrow as I made through today. As I prepare for rest, I ask for Your blessings upon me and others in the area of rest and sleep.

Lord, I know that rest is one of Your gifts, and I thank You for the opportunity to pause and renew. I ask that You calm my mind, ease my heart, and help me to release the worries of the day into Your hands. Remind me that You are in control and that I can rest securely in Your care.

Be with my friends and family tonight, Lord—those I talk to and those I don't. Bless those who are restless, anxious, or in need of Your peace. May Your presence comfort them and remind them they are never alone. Let my rest be peaceful and restorative so that I may wake up ready to walk in Your purpose tomorrow.

Lord, thank You for showing me Your Grace, Love, Mercy, and Generosity. Help me to always show the light of You to everyone I meet and encounter so that they know that what I do is not of me but You working through me.

In the name of Your Holy Mighty Son Jesus, Amen.

Prayer for Energy and Strength to Thrive

Dear Heavenly Father, I humbly come before You to thank You for this day. I don't take it lightly that You've blessed me with the gift of life and another opportunity to serve You. I ask for Your guidance and strength as I navigate the area of energy today.

Lord, I acknowledge that You are the source of all vitality and strength. I ask that You renew my body and spirit, giving me the energy I need to fulfill my responsibilities and serve others with joy. When I feel weary, remind me to turn to You for rest and refreshment.

I also lift up those who are drained, physically or emotionally. Be their strength and their peace, Lord. Show them that they can lean on You when their energy is spent. Help me to use my energy wisely and prioritize the tasks and relationships that glorify You.

Dear Lord, I ask for forgiveness for my shortcomings today. Be with those who need You—those who call on You and those who don't. Bless my friends, my family, and anyone who crosses my path.

Lord, thank You for showing me Your Grace, Love, Mercy, and Generosity. Help me to always show the light of You to everyone I meet and encounter so that they know that what I do is not of me but You working through me.

In the name of Your Holy Mighty Son Jesus, Amen.

Prayer for Health, Fitness, and Wellness

Dear Heavenly Father, I humbly come before You to thank You for this day. I don't take it for granted that You've given me this body and the ability to move, breathe, and live. As I go through this day, please guide me to make wise decisions in the area of fitness, health, and wellness.

Lord, I ask for strength and discipline to take care of the temple You've entrusted to me. Help me to nourish my body with the right foods, stay active to build strength, and rest when I need to. Protect me from illness, injury, and unhealthy habits, and guide me in living a life that honors the gift of health You've given me.

I also pray for those who are struggling with their health. Be their healer and their strength, Lord. Show them that You are with them every step of their journey. Let my journey of health and wellness be a testimony to Your goodness, and may it inspire others to seek You in all areas of their lives.

Lord, thank You for showing me Your Grace, Love, Mercy, and Generosity. Help me to always show the light of You to everyone I meet and encounter so that they know that what I do is not of me but You working through me.

In the name of Your Holy Mighty Son Jesus, Amen.

Prayer for Confidence in Physical Appearance

Dear Lord, I humbly come before You to thank You for this day. I'm so grateful for the body You've given me and the unique ways You've created me. I ask that You help me to see, recognize, and celebrate Your blessings in the area of physical appearance.

Lord, help me to see myself through Your eyes—as someone who is fearfully and wonderfully made. Teach me to care for my body with love and respect, knowing it is a temple of the Holy Spirit. Guard me against insecurities or comparisons, and fill me with confidence that comes from knowing my true worth is in You.

Be with those who struggle with how they see themselves, Lord. Help them to feel Your love and to recognize their beauty and value in Your eyes. Let me be a reflection of Your love and light to those who may be in need of encouragement today.

Lord, thank You for showing me Your Grace, Love, Mercy, and Generosity. Help me to always show the light of You to everyone I meet and encounter so that they know that what I do is not of me but You working through me.

In the name of Your Holy Mighty Son Jesus, Amen.

WRITTEN BY:

Cecelia Fay Morris

THE DIGITAL MARKETING MAVEN

Cecelia is the Owner and Founder of Taking Charge, Inc. a Digital Marketing Agency. She is the Digital Media Marketing Manager for Thriving Women Network, Inc., an internet broadcast company on e360tv.com.

She has helped network marketers and online businessbuilders stay current and relevant on social media to generate hundreds of thousands of qualified leads, clients, customers, and sales without relying on only organic marketing and the ever-changing algorithms. Most recently she has been a SCORE business mentor and a contributor to the Economic & Community Development Institute (ECDI).

(f) biohackyourhappy

God Is Sovereign

"FOR I KNOW THE PLANS I HAVE FOR YOU,
DECLARES THE LORD, PLANS FOR WELFARE
AND NOT FOR EVIL, TO GIVE YOU A FUTURE
AND A HOPE."
(JEREMIAH 29:11)

Healing Through Trust and Faith

Father God,

In times of struggle, when the weight of life feels unbearable, we come before You, seeking Your comfort and peace. Remind us, Lord, that even in the darkest valleys, You walk beside us. Though we may not understand the purpose of our pain, we trust that You are using it to strengthen and shape us.

When doubts creep in, assure us of Your presence. You are our refuge when all else feels uncertain. Help us lean on You, trusting that You are working all things for our good. Give us the courage to surrender our fears and rest in Your wisdom.

Grant us the strength to rise above trials and rebuild from broken places. Heal us—body, mind, and spirit—and fill our hearts with peace. May we find hope in the journey and joy in Your lessons.

We trust in Your love, healing, and perfect timing. Thank You for holding us close. In Jesus' name, Amen.

"And we know that in all things God works for the good of those who love him, who have been called according to his purpose." – Romans 8:28

Prayer for Parkinson's Disease

Father God,

We come to You, carrying the weight of Parkinson's disease. The trembling hands, unsteady steps, and daily challenges can feel overwhelming, but we trust that You see us and care deeply for each of us. Lord, we ask for Your healing touch. Steady our bodies, calm our minds, and ease the fear and frustration that sometimes fill our hearts.

Strengthen us to face each day and give us the courage to trust in Your perfect plan. Surround us with compassionate doctors who understand our needs and loved ones who support us through this journey. Help us to feel Your presence with every step, even when the path feels difficult.

We know You are our strength and refuge. When we stumble, remind us that You are holding us up. May Your peace fill our hearts, and may Your love carry us forward, one moment at a time. Amen.

"The Lord makes firm the steps of the one who delights in him; though he may stumble, he will not fall, for the Lord upholds him with his hand." – Psalm 37:23-24

Prayer for Autoimmune Diseases

Father God,

We come to You, seeking healing and restoration for our bodies. Living with autoimmune diseases is a daily battle, but we trust in Your power to bring balance and peace. Lord, restore harmony to our immune systems, ease the inflammation, and renew our strength.

When the pain and fatigue overwhelm us, fill us with Your peace and courage. Help us to trust that You are with us in every moment. Guide the hands of our doctors and caregivers, giving them wisdom and insight to provide the care we need. Surround us with loved ones who will encourage and support us in this journey.

Lord, remind us that we are fearfully and wonderfully made. Even in our struggles, we trust in Your promise to heal and restore. Let us find hope in Your unfailing love and joy in the knowledge that You are working all things for our good. Amen.

"But I will restore you to health and heal your wounds,' declares the Lord." – Jeremiah 30:17

Prayer for Fibromyalgia

Father God,

We come to You, weary from the constant pain and exhaustion of fibromyalgia. Lord, we ask for Your healing touch. Relieve our aching bodies, restore our energy, and grant us peaceful sleep that renews our strength and spirit.

When we feel unseen or misunderstood, remind us that You know our every struggle. Guide us to treatments and care that will bring relief and peace. Bless those who care for us, giving them compassion and patience as they walk with us through this journey.

Help us to find joy even in small victories and moments of rest. Strengthen our spirits when the days feel overwhelming, and calm our anxious hearts with Your peace. Remind us that we are never alone, for You are walking with us every step of the way. We trust in Your love and faithfulness, which never fail. Amen.

"Come to me, all you who are weary and burdened, and I will give you rest." – Matthew 11:28

Prayer for Reproductive System Health

Father God,

We come to You, seeking healing for our reproductive health. For those of us living with pain or struggling with infertility, we ask for Your restorative touch. Heal our bodies, bring balance to our hormones, and ease the burdens we carry.

For those of us longing to conceive, grant us patience and peace as we wait on Your perfect timing. For those grieving loss or unmet hopes, wrap us in Your comforting embrace. Guide our doctors and caregivers with wisdom and skill to provide the care we need.

Help us to trust Your plan, even when it feels unclear. Remind us that we are beautifully and wonderfully made in Your image. May Your truth replace our fears with hope, and may Your love fill us with strength and grace. We place our healing and our trust in Your hands, Lord. Amen.

"He settles the childless woman in her home as a happy mother of children. Praise the Lord." – Psalm 113:9

WRITTEN BY:

Nancy Clark

NURSE NANCY / CERTIFIED SELF-LEADERSHIP COACH

Nancy Clark, MSN, RN, Certified AI Consultant, and Certified Self-Leadership Coach, combines over 20 years of nursing expertise with a mission to empower others. As the founder of AIsezz and Pure Imagination Consulting, she simplifies complex concepts and fosters personal and professional growth through workshops and coaching.

Nancy's approach blends technical knowledge, motivational guidance, and a deep commitment to authenticity and healing, helping individuals thrive and achieve their fullest potential. She is passionate about fostering wellness, hope, and positivity in every aspect of life.

- www.linkedin.com/in/nancy-clark-consultant
- pureimaginationconsulting.com

God Is Our Shield

"EVERY WORD OF GOD PROVES TRUE; HE IS A
SHIELD TO THOSE WHO TAKE REFUGE IN
HIM."
(PROVERBS 30:5)

Divine Healing
Isaiah 53:5

Father God, in the Name of Jesus, I Declare and Decree By the Divine Healing of the Stripes of Jesus we are Healed.

Every part of my Body will encompass the Divine Healing of Jesus Christ. No diabetes, low or high sugar, high blood pressure, any type of cancer, strokes, or heart attack will come nigh our dwelling. Nothing will be able to attack our Blood types in Jesus' name. Every organ in our Body will line up with the Word of God according to Psalms 139:14, and because we are fearfully and wonderfully made, we will reject any sickness, and we will come against any malfunction in our body in Jesus' name.

By your Word, Lord God, every spirit of infirmity will be uprooted and consumed by the power of the Holy Spirit and the Anointing. Lord God, you bore our Healing on your Body; you took on our infirmities that we can have Divine Healing from the Top of our Heads to the Souls of our Feet.

Allow your Word to manifest a complete Divine Healing physically, spiritually, and emotionally in Jesus' name. As we stand upon and walk in the Divine Healing by the Grace and the Sovereignty of the Messiah, Jesus Christ.

Amen.

Divine Healing According to Psalms 103:3

Father God, in the Name of Jesus, I come before you Humbly and with great Confidence thanking you for your Divine Healing of all diseases from the top of our Heads to the Souls of our Feet. Father, you said for us to ask and you Hear us, so Father, I am asking for Complete Divine Healing in Our Body in Jesus' Name: Restored Strength, Enhanced Stamina, Igniting our Minds, Illuminating our Spirits, and Provoking that vitality in our total Being as we trust you in Jesus' name.

Father, wrap your loving Arms around us as we walk through our Healing. Lord God, Manifest your Healing power and rejuvenate our Body so we fill your Divine Healing Virtue Flowing through us in Jesus' name.

Father God, as your Divine Healing flows through us, Touch our minds so that we comprehend and understand your Word. Heal and open our Ear Gates that we hear you Clearly, and Heal our Eye Gates, Lord God, that we see correctly. Because our Bodies are your Temple, Lord God, we thank you that no sickness, disease, nor plagues will come upon us in Jesus' name, and they do not have access because we are covered by your Blood of Jesus.

So we Declare our Divine Healing as we pray this prayer by Faith in Jesus' name.

Divine Armour of Healing

Father God, in the name of Jesus, I come thanking you for Divine Good Health in our Bodies. Thank You for Our Sound Minds Being Healed of every negative thought, just like the woman who touched the Hem of your garment, and she was healed. We touch you, Lord God, with our Prayer, Praise, and Worship, and Divine Healing begins to flow through our Body, Soul, and Spirit.

Our testimony of Divine Healing is The Armor of The Word that protects and provides the covering of our Heart with the breastplate of righteousness, peace that covers our feet (walk), our loins are Girded with Divine Healing of Truth in the Word of God, our Minds are covered with the Divine Healing of Salvation.

Then we put on the Whole Armour of God so we can stand against any Sickness and Disease with the Shield of Faith in the Divine Healing of God's Word as we yield our total Self to God's Healing Virtue. We Declare and Decree that the Spirit of Lord's Divine Healing will Manifest within our Whole Body, that we Walk victorious in our Healing in Jesus' name.

As we worship You, El ROI who sees, and JEHOVAH RAPHA / YHWH RAPHA, THE LORD THAT HEALS, IN JESUS' NAME, Amen.

Divine Healing in the Secret Place - Psalms 91:4

Father God, in the name of Jesus, thank you for allowing me to dwell in the secret place of my Divine Healing where no noisome pestilence can harm us. We thank you for your Shield and Buckler that covers us from the snare and the fowler. You are a place of Refuge when we need a Healing, and we can hide under your wings of Divine Healing because of you being that Balm in Gilead so we don't have to be afraid of the terror of any Sickness and disease or the fear of any arrows that try to harm us. The arrow shall fail, and it won't prosper according to your Word; it won't come close to us at all.

Because we are your Daughter, your Word, Lord God, tells us that you will Set us on High because we know who you are, and we know your name, and your Name is Jehovah Rapha, the God that Healeth Thee.

If we abide under your Wings of Protection, Lord, you will give us the satisfaction of long life and Divine Healing and your Love for us, your people. We will continue to be blessed and walk triumphant in Victory and Divine Healing - Mind, Body, and Spirit.

Father, we will not fret because of the evilness of the enemy trying to put any type of sickness upon us because you are Jehovah Rohi, the Lord our Shepherd, who causes us to lay down in Green Pastures of Divine Healing. As we continue to walk in our Healing, you become our Light and Banner, and our Life becomes a Living Epistle and Testimony of being Healed by Yahweh Elohim (The Lord God).

Declaration of Divine Healing Prayer

Father God, in the name of Jesus, we come before you this morning honoring Who you are as The Divine Healer of Everything. You are the only one that has the Power to Heal according to your Word because you are the All-Seeing, All-Knowing, and All-Powerful God that created the universe and formed man from the dust of the ground and woman from man's rib and breathed into the nostrils of man, and man became a living soul.

So as we come to Declare and Decree Divine Healing according to your Word by Faith in Jesus' name, I Declare and Decree my Divine Healing according to Isaiah 53:5: *"Where your wounds you bore and the 39 stripes that covered your back for Our Healing and the bruises you received for us to be Whole and Have Life Abundantly."*

We say thank you for being a Shepherd that watches to make sure her sheep are well and safe from danger. I Declare that You, YHWH, being The One Who is Self-Existent, the One who Paid the Price with your Life, that we could Have a Totally Complete Divine Life in You.

In Jesus' name, Amen.

WRITTEN BY:

Apostle Dr. Shannon Hall

SPECIAL EDUCATION TEACHER, ORDAINED PASTOR

Dr. Shannon Hall has been married for 15 years. She has 2 children and was born and raised in Orlando, Florida. The family now resides in Atlanta, Georgia, where Dr. Shannon Hall currently works for Dekalb County School as a Pre-K Special Education Teacher. Dr. Shannon Hall was called to the ministry in 1990.

In 1992, she joined Holy Tabernacles Church of Deliverance under Lewis I. Nicholson Senior, where she accepted her calling. It was there that she met her spiritual mother, Elder Elaine Lewis, who introduced her to Pastor Rosie E. Bess. Dr. Hall then served as an evangelist under her tutelage at the Independent Church of God, where she served until 2001. Dr. Hall transitioned to Georgia under God's guidance and instruction, where she participated in various ministries. She was ordained as a pastor while serving under Apostles Barbra and Leon Beeler. Additionally, Dr. Hall was part of the ministerial staff of Wings of Faith Ministries under the tutelage of Bishop Dreyfus Smith. She also served as an oversight pastor at Kingdom Living Ministries.

The scripture given to her by God was Romans 5:5:
"Now hope does not disappoint, because the love of God has been poured out in our hearts by the Holy Spirit who was given to us." Also Luke 4:18:
"The Spirit of the Lord is upon me, because he hath anointed me to preach the gospel to the poor; he hath sent me to heal the brokenhearted, to preach deliverance to the captives, and recovering of sight to the blind, to set at liberty them that are bruised."

In 2018 she founded "Women Walking Victoriously." On May 2021, Dr. Hall was affirmed as an apostle by Apostle Renaldo Turner in South Carolina and reaffirmed by Apostle Groves by the laying of hands and pouring of oil on June 4, 2022. Now she is currently a part of (KRIM) Kingdom Remnant International Ministries, where the presiding prelate is Apostle Alee Groves, and where she went through her consecration and anointing. Dr. Shannon Hall has accomplished great work.

God Is Eternal

"THE ETERNAL GOD IS YOUR DWELLING
PLACE, AND UNDERNEATH ARE THE
EVERLASTING ARMS."
(DEUTERONOMY 33:27)

Trusting in Your Purpose: A Prayer of Gratitude

F ather God,

Might we express gratitude for the daily manifestation of abundance that You provide us with? Allow Yourself to continue to be our guiding force, bestowing upon us strength and wisdom to accomplish Your purpose while nurturing our inner selves. We understand, however, that we are utterly helpless without You, Holy Father.

Your Excellency, please grant us the opportunity to uplift all our family members, friends, and believers who never loosen their grip on You. Lord, help those who see darkness closing in around them. Speak to them what they desperately seek to hear—you are loved and always will be.

With every challenge, each breath becomes heavier than the last. Father, please hear these broken cries; restore them. Shield my praying friends with the Holy Spirit, protecting them from every burden that haunts their being. May they see You and feel Your presence in their deepest pain; in that moment, there is no need for words.

Mighty Father, I beseech You to always keep us safe in every aspect of our lives. Let Your protection surround us, and may we depend on Your Word for our daily needs. Assist us in being Your peacemakers, spreading good works and love to those around us.

We know there are unknowns and difficulties to face. Remind us to wait upon You and to remember that all things work according to Your purpose. Grant us tenderness in our hearts and clarity in our minds so that even in extreme situations, we will respond with grace.

Thank You, Lord, for Your never-ending love and support. May we always seek Your wisdom in our decisions and find strength in Your Word. We place our lives in Your hands, trusting that You will lead us on the right path.

Prayer for a Breadwinner

Heavenly Father,

I approach you with a sorrowing spirit and a collapsed soul so that you may guide my efforts and defend me as the head of my household. I took the liberty to thank You for the roles that You have given me and also for the means to sustain those that are dear to my heart because I understand that any means of provision can only come from You, Lord.

My Lord, give me the understanding to balance our resources. May all my choices glorify You. I put my family first because I know that they require my complete satisfaction, not just physically but emotionally and spiritually as well.

Let's not forget about the challenges and tiredness of doing any work. I want to do this work even more and with all my heart. Make me remember that I do not work in vain because my job is for my family and You, Lord! Even the defeated path remains intact. I ask God to stay inspired and continue to work as best I can.

I want to pray that my family is in harmony in whatever place they may be and in whatever condition they may be in. Protect them wherever they may walk or be so that our house may be filled with your love and joy. Let them be comfortable around me, and let that parting be an emotional overcoming event for me because I do so as I attempt to keep them safe.

I also beg You, Lord, for assistance when I'm in doubt. When financial stress is bound to come or if there are interruptions, let me not forget to have faith in Your help. Remind me to rely on You and to search for Your counsel in each other.

May my efforts not only sustain my family but also serve as a testimony of Your goodness and faithfulness. Let my work be a source of inspiration to others, demonstrating that with hard work and faith in You, all things are possible.

Thank You, Lord, for being our ultimate provider. I place my family and my responsibilities in Your loving hands, trusting that You will lead us through every trial and triumph.

In Jesus' name, I pray. Amen.

Healing Prayer for Those Suffering from Illness

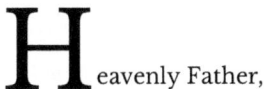

Heavenly Father,

We come before You as sad people. Remember all those who are looking for help in all ways but are unable to do so due to illness or economic constraints. We understand and know that You are the Great Physician, and we are comfortable committing to Your healing hands any and every individual who seems to be in contact with so much pain and suffering.

Lord, You know what is best for these individuals. They give strength and hope to so many. Bless them with Your divine healing. Protect them, be with them in their difficult moments. When they seem distant, let them feel Your presence, full of love. Let what is beyond comprehension, Your peace, be their shield as they battle their adverse health situation.

We also remember those who could not afford to pay the bills for healthcare: Lord, open doors for them. Let them have the facilities that may assist them in the prayers that will help them be eased back into health. Let them be amply able to be received with favorable and generous conditions in their situations.

Father, we also pray for their families and caregivers, asking them to be headstrong and motivated. Endow them with the strength to sustain their destitute in hard moments and fill their hearts with optimism. Assist them in focusing their thoughts on the fulfillment of Your will for them and not on the current problems.

Lord, we believe in the power of faith and prayer. We ask for Your miraculous touch upon the ill, transforming their situations from impossible to possible. Let their healing be a testament to Your goodness and mercy.

Thank You, Lord, for hearing our prayers. We trust in Your unfailing love and the hope that You bring to our lives. May all who suffer know that they are not alone, and may they find comfort in Your promises.

In Jesus' name, we pray.
Amen.

Prayer for the Success of the Business and the Team

Heavenly Father,

We appreciate your wisdom and guidance. First of all, we are grateful for the chance to be part of this business and work with a committed team. Every achievement is a product of God's favor, and we work in accordance with His will.

In order to proceed, we would like to pray. We want your help in achieving growth in our business. Allow it to blossom within the framework of Your Paradise. Realistically, it helps us in our decisions, makes us creative in our strategies, and makes us honest in what we do. Help us serve our clients, customers, and communities in such a way that our work represents your love through the quality of our services.

We would also like to pray for our team members. We want to start by uniting us together and focalizing our work towards mutual collaboration. Let us help each other and work together with peace and understanding. Let us come up with synergistic results where our input combined would equal far more than what we would have achieved while operating as separate individuals.

In times of adversity and doubt, help us remember to turn to You for support. Focus our attention on what increases our motivation, and use us as instruments of Change, working relentlessly until the last minute, even in the face of the impossible.

Father, we humbly request your support for all our plans. Please allow us to have access to business opportunities that lead to beneficial partnerships and prospects. We should be able to make a difference with our efforts not only in our business but also in the society where we operate.

Lastly, instill in us a spirit of gratitude and humility. May we always give thanks for our achievements and acknowledge that our success reflects Your goodness.

Thank You, Lord, for Your unwavering support and guidance. We place our business and our team in Your capable hands, trusting that You will lead us on the path to success.

In Jesus' name, we pray.
Amen.

WRITTEN BY:

Clarita Reyes
CREATIVE CANVA DESIGNER

Clarita Reyes is a results-oriented professional with extensive experience in remote administrative and back-office operations. With a robust background in importation and purchasing, she is adept at streamlining business processes and enhancing operational efficiency.

Clarita is committed to delivering exceptional service and solutions to clients, whether through full-time or part-time engagements.

From 2019 to 2024, she held the position of Remote Manager at CCI, an esteemed import business and marketing agency operating in Singapore and the Philippines. In this role, Clarita expertly oversaw the coordination of import operations and the execution of marketing strategies from a remote environment. She was instrumental in managing logistics and inventory, ensuring seamless operations and timely product delivery. Her innovative marketing campaigns significantly elevated brand visibility and drove sales growth for various imported products.

Since 2024, Clarita has transitioned to Sunday Enterprises as their Creative Designer. Passionate about creating impactful designs, she leverages her expertise to produce visually compelling content that resonates with target audiences and aligns with the company's strategic objectives. Clarita feels blessed and grateful to be part of the Sunday Enterprises team, where she can fully express her creativity and contribute to the company's success.

Known for her dedication, reliability, and proactive approach, Clarita is passionate about empowering clients to achieve their goals and continuously seeks opportunities to contribute to organizational success in a remote working environment.

The Gratitude Mandate: God's Will for a Thankful Heart

Father God, I come with a heart bursting with gratitude celebrating You, our Sovereign Lord, who blessed me with another year as your Dunamis Daughter endowed with your Exousia Power for Your Kingdom Purpose.

Lord, I ask that You grant every person reading this with Your Anointing to fulfill their indivdual Kingdom assignments for Your Kingdom Glory. Knowing that the Gratitude Mandate is Your will for us to have a Thankful heart, as Paul wrote in 1 Thessalonians 5:18, "To Give Thanks in ALL Things." May we embrace the following 5 P's as we quest to be doers of Your Holy Word for Your Perfect Plan and Purpose.

1. Lord, please allow us to create SPACE to dwell in your Presence. Psalm 95.2.
2. Create a hunger and thirst for your Word that we will sit and Ponder Passages with Thanksgiving. Psalm 100:4
3. May we Practice gratitude by journaling and sharing daily blessings. Psalm 9:1
4. Father God, allow us to offer Praise and Prayers of Thanksgiving in ALL Things. Psalm 95:2-3
5. Finally, Lord, please guide us to Places where People's hearts illuminate your grace. Colossians 3:16-17

In Christ Jesus Name, Amen.

WRITTEN BY:

Dr. Glenda Bailey Hayden

AUTHOR, SPEAKER, COACH, AND FOUNDER OF EXOUSIA TRANSFORMATION SPACE, LLC

Dr. Glenda Bailey Hayden, Author, Speaker, Coach, and Founder of Exousia Transformation Space, LLC, transforms family dynamics from ordinary to "Kingdomstrodinary."

With a Doctorate in Christian Counseling and 20+ years as a Licensed Clinician, she empowers families to embrace their God-given authority to create Kingdom S.P.A.C.E.—Stillness, Presence, Awareness, to Confidently Execute.

A New Orleans native, proud mother, and joyful 'God-Glamma,' Dr. Hayden blends professional expertise with her passion for the Word, travel, and dance to foster legacies of freedom and spiritual renewal.

- (f) @drgbhayden
- (ig) @drgbhayden
- (in) linkedin.com/in/glenda-b-hayden
- (🌐) drglendahayden.com

God Is Just

"THE ROCK, HIS WORK IS PERFECT, FOR ALL
HIS WAYS ARE JUSTICE. A GOD OF
FAITHFULNESS AND WITHOUT INIQUITY, JUST
AND UPRIGHT IS HE."
(DEUTERONOMY 32:4)

John 16:33

John 16:33
"These things I have spoken to you that in the you may have peace. In the world, you will have tribulation, But be a good cheer I have overcome the world"

Father God, thank you for the peace that passes all understanding. We know that no matter what you will never stop fighting for us when hardship enters our lives. With each step today give us clarity in our choices and decisions.

May you shine your peace on our troubled minds and remove the shackles of disorder and frustration from our circumstances. May we trust your steps that you lead us and may we depend on you with all of our being that peace is with is and our minds are clear.

In Jesus name Amen.

Guard Your Heart

Proverbs 4:23
  Above all else guard your heart for everything you do flows from it.

Father God,

Today I pray that you guard the hearts of those who may be battling decisions. I ask that you help us know that you are near and will help guide us to the pathway of your purpose.

I pray that the distraction will not prevail, and that focus is centered on the direction that will help protect and show us the way of your light in dark places.

 I pray that when people places and things lead us down a road of disobedience, may we turn back to you and trust you with all our hearts and may you give us wisdom knowledge and understandin.

AMEN.

Fleeing from Temptation

Matthew 26:41
Watch and pray so that you will not fall into temptation. The spirit is willing, but the flesh is weak.

Father God, although our spirit wants to do right at times, our flesh falls into weakness. I ask that you help us who are weak to not fall into temptation and to be strong mentally in our mind to line up with our spirit.

When we are weak show us your strength and send us someone to help us overcome our weaknesses until we can manage them ourselves. Thank you, Jesus, for helping us recognize the temptation. Thank you for loving us to show us the clear path and to forgive us when we mess up and fall down in our mistakes.

May we seek you and be guided by scriptures to know right from wrong. May you convict out hearts even before we act on the sin itself and give you praise in advance for helping is see clearly through troubled waters, Amen.

Memories of Abuse

Philippians 4:13
I can do all things in Him who give me strength.

Father God help us to have to courage to be bold and brave to overcome the negative memories of abuse and to know your desire is for us to use our experiences to be helpful to someone else.

Help us to live a purpose filled life taking our past situations and using them to glorify you through being the positive example. Thank you for clearing our mind from bad emotions and not letting them control us anymore.

Set us free from the bondage of bad memories of abuse. Thank you seeing that we are free to love again and not be affected by the residue of our past abuse. Amen.

Pushing Through The Pain

Proverbs 18:10
The name of the Lord is a strong tower the righteous run into it and are safe.

Father God, please help us to acknowledge the pain in our life and deal with it. We ask that you help us see that we cannot handle alone.

We ask that you help us to know that we can run to you as our safe tower to overcome our fears and to get the comfort we need.

Even when times are hard, we know we can trust you for support and safety. Thank you, God, for helping us to push through the pain. Amen.

WRITTEN BY:

Robin Shockley

VISIONARY, BLOGGER, MEDIA PUBLICIST, COMMUNITY ADVOCATE, SPEAKER, TALKSHOW HOST, AUTHOR & ACTRESS

As the Founder of " Focus Forward with Robin ", she is a Columnist Writer for several magazines, Professional Maximizer Awards Director pand Ambassador of the Sports Karate Museum, International Ambassador Come on In Inc., Visionary Servant-Leader Coach, Entrepreneur, Media Publicist, Theatre & Film Actress, Talk Show Host, Community & Domestic Violence Advocate, Motivational Speaker and Food Blogger/ Talent & Pageantry Judge as well as Published Author and writer of over 60 inspiring faith base devotionals.

Robin host events & serves the community by bringing women together sharing access skills and advocacy.

Robin's purpose is being the link between a person who needs help and those who help; Motivating people to recognize their Potential and Purpose for moving forward while living their best legacy today through serving others. As the Founder of Girls Gifted 4 God, she serves her community facilitating Vision Board Workshops, speaking events, and providing a platform for others to build their brand.

Recently in 2023 she created the Swift Magazine platform to empower over thirty plus women & men across the country to write their stories to help single women stay in focus today through self-defense techniques, beauty tips cooking recipes, an inspirational true to life stories.

While Interviewing for Social Media & Magazines for others to share their "WHY" story, she is the bridge maker that inspires small businesses to gain confidence to recognize the importance of stepping forward to make a difference for future generations. Contact Robin Shockley to speak, perform, host or facilitate your next event @ Swiftmagazine22@gmail.com

 www.robinshockley.com

God Is Compassionate

"THE LORD IS GRACIOUS AND RIGHTEOUS;
OUR GOD IS FULL OF COMPASSION."
(PSALM 116:5)

Warfare of the Mind

"28 Come to me come all who are weary and heavy burden and I will give you rest take my yoke upon you and learn from me for I am gentle and humble in heart and you will find rest(renewal, blessed quiet) for your souls. 30 For my yoke is easy and my burden is light.
Matthew 11:28-30

Dear Lord

My days and nights are sometimes blurred into one big fog. I try to figure out which direction to go but things just become blurred. The more I try to figure out my life it's just becomes one big maze filled with confusion and regret. My life is like a hamster on a wheel I'm just going around and around with no end in sight. My mind is racing with thoughts of anger rage, sadness, hopelessness, peace, love, joy and confusion over and over again. This maze has me going crazy and doubting who you created me to be. I can't see clear path and whatever clarity I have is quickly fading away. Lord what should I do? This depression won't subside. Lord I need you now to heal, deliver and restore my mind. These feeling of depression are taking over my mind, body, and soul.

In your word you said you inhabit the praises of your people I will praise you Lord and lay my burdens on you. I will not worry or fret about the many unanswered questions in my life for I know you have the answers and in due time you will reveal them to me. I will put on the garment of praise for the spirit of heaviness.

According to Daniel 2: 22 -23 it is he who reveals the profound and hidden things he knows what is in the darkness and the light dwells with him. I thank you and praise you oh God of my father's.

For you have given me wisdom and power even now, you have made known to me what we requested of you. For you have made known to us (the solution) it's the King's matter.

Lord you said to cast all our cares upon you for you care for us and will provide all our needs. I will trust you and stay connected to your word. I will walk by faith and not by sight. Lord I thank you for loving me and teaching me to cast all my cares on you and to rest in the perfect peace that only you can give. This prayer I seal with my most holy faith and I receive your love today.

In Jesus name
Amen

Gynecological Health

25 A woman in the crowd had suffered from a hemorrhage for 12 years 26 and had endured much suffering at the hands of many physicians. She had spent all that she had and was not helped at all but instead had become worse. 27 She had heard reports about Jesus and she came up behind him in the crowd and touched his outer robe. 28 For she thought, "if I just touched his clothing I will get well". 29 Immediately her flow of blood was dried up; and she felt in her body and knew without any doubt that she was healed of suffering. Immediately Jesus, recognizing in Himself that power had gone from Him, turned around in the crowd and asked, "Who touched my clothes?" 30 His disciples said to him, "You see the crowd is pressing in around you from all sides, and you ask "Who touched me?" 32 Still he kept looking around to see the woman who had done it. 33 And the woman, though she was afraid and trembling, aware of what had happened to her came and fell down before him and told him the whole truth. 34 Then he said to her, "Daughter, your faith your personal trust and confidence in me has restored you to health; go in peace and be permanently healed from your suffering".
Mark 5:25-34

As a woman I have often struggled with the same issues as the woman with the issue of blood. My journey with gynecological issues started at a young age I started my menstrual cycle in the 4th grade and Lord you know pain and embarrassment I felt. Then as a young adult I didn't even know I had to go see a gynecologist when I became sexually active. In my house female issues were never talked about nor sex. I had so many scares with abnormal pap tests and excessive bleeding. There were so many mysteries to the female body, I felt I needed a four year degree to figure it out (lol) I know many of my sisters have had the same issues and can identify with my pain.

My prayer is that God will restore our reproductive system uterus, ovaries, fallopian tubes and cervix. I believe God for total healing and restoration for my sisters. God your word said we are healed from all sickness and disease through your son Jesus Christ. By his stripes we are healed and healing is our birthright.

I plead the blood of Jesus over my sister's and against irregular periods an excessive monthly blood flow. God I know you did this for the woman with the issue of blood and I know you can do it for your daughters. I plead the blood of Jesus against ovarian cyst, fibroids and cervical cancer all of these elements must cease in Jesus name.

For my sisters who had miscarriages and loss of life. Your womb is not barren you can still bring life into this world again. You are the apple of God's eye and no good thing will he withhold from his daughters, who love the Lord.

For all the women reading this message I pray that all gynecological issues will be resolved and everything in your reproductive system will line up with the word of God and work accordingly to how God designed it to be. Any gynecological issue that would try to plague your reproductive system will return to the pit of hell and never come back , in Jesus name.

To my sisters who want to be moms I pray God will continue to fill your hearts with a mothers love and that passion you have to become a mom, God will bring it to fruition. Lord I pray you make childbirth easy for them and that they will have healthy whole beautiful babies, that they will teach Godly principles . I thank you God for being the ultimate healer and loving your daughters, for we know we are truly the apple of your eye and we are fearfully and wonderfully made. I seal this prayer with my most holy faith. In Jesus name, Amen.

Strongholds of the Mind

4 The weapons we fight with are not the weapons of the world. On the contrary, they have divine power to demolish strongholds. 5 We demolish arguments and every pretension that sets itself up against the knowledge of God, and we take captive every thought to make it obedient to christ. 6 And we will be ready to punish every act of disobedience, once your obedience is complete.
2 Corinthians 10:4-6

El Shaddai (God Almighty) I need you today. As I go through life I strive to overcome Obstacles and avoid the pitfalls that seem to be ever so present in my life. I find myself worrying about the pain of my past and what the future will hold. I worry about if I will fulfill the purpose you have on my life. My goal is to leave everything in this world that you put in me. But my thinking keeps me in trap, there have been so many patterns of abuse, neglect and self-destruction that keeps me bound. Lord, my behaviors don't reflect the bountiful blessings that you have given me instead my actions are destructive and lead me down paths that are no good for my soul. These strongholds ruin the very essence of who you called me to be, and these strongholds go from generation to generation, repeating there course of destruction.

These strongholds are spiritual not physical. Like Paul said there is a thorn in my side that causes me to do wrong when I want to do right. The battle of good vs evil continues to rage within my soul. El Shaddai continue to give me the strength to take every though captive with what your word said about me. Lord help me walk in the fruits of the spirit, love, joy, peace, patience, gentleness and self-control (Gal 5:22-23).

God I want to live as a reflection of your love on this earth. The same love that Christ exhibited when he walked the earth. Agape love of Christ, the highest, purest and unconditional form of love.

I pray that the strongholds will be broken in Jesus name. I will walk in freedom and liberty. I declare and degree that I will be reverse generational curses and strongholds in my family. I will life my life on purpose and according to your will. The next generation in my family will never know the depts of sin and mental anguish I've endured. I break every chain from my mind and every curse that would try to stand against the word of God. I John 4:4 said greater is he that's in me, than he that's in the world. I take authority over the enemy and declare the word of God over my life. Lord, I give you total control over my lie . Your will be done and not mine, I put you first and surrender all to you.

My family will produce generation of Godly men and women that walk-in power and authority and change the generations to come. My family will be restored to wholeness and peace. For me and my house we will serve the lord (Joshua 24:15) I seal this prayer with my most holy faith.

In Jesus name, Amen

"Eloi, Eloi, lema sabachthaniana?"

34 And at three in the afternoon Jesus Cried out in a loud voice, "Eloi, Eloi, lema sabacthtani" (which means "My God ,my God, why have you forsaken me?")
Mark 15:34

Can you imagine leaving your throne, to come down to earth and die for a world filled with sin. Can you imagine your heavenly father leaving you, dying on the cross. Your heavenly father who has all power in his hand and can do anything. However, he needs you to become the sacrifice, you are the sacrificial lamb to save the world. Before Christ people were worshiping idol gods, falsehoods and all types of religions. This world was lost and in need of a savior. Jesus took the burdens of this world and he put them on his back and he bleed and died for you and me.. He did not want to do this, he asked GOD if this cup could be passed from him but, he decided Lord your will not my will be done.

Jesus felt forsaken ,he felt the pain of not being loved, and betrayed. Christ had the power to save himself , but he died so that you and I can walk in victory. There is no disease that Jesus cannot heal. There is no pain, there is no sorrow, that Jesus did not feel. His sacrifice changed the trajectory of this world and every generation that would come after. I know you may be feeling discouraged and that no one cares but understand there is a savior who died for you and gave up his heavenly throne for you. If you were the only person in this world he would have done it for you .

My prayer for you today is that you walk in the victory and the knowledge of God a loving father, and his son Jesus Christ our savior who died for you. Through his death he gave us power over the enemy.He went to hell and got the keys, from the devil so you never have to live a defeatist lifestyle. My hope is that you stand up and say I am a child of God, I am the righteousness of God,. I was bought with a price and I'm worthy of Gods love and grace. Greater is he that is in me ,than he that's in the world 1 John4:14.

Every gift and purpose God has given you will manifest in your life and you will exceed the goal.

If you don't know this God I speak of repeat this prayer with me, For God so loved the world that he gave his only begotten son and whosoever believeth in him shall not perish but have everlasting life John 3:16. If you believe that with your heart and you confess with your mouth you are saved. The same power that rests in Christ is within you now *12"Very truly I tell you, whoever believes in me will do the works I have been doing, and they will do even greater things because I am going to the father"13 And I will do whatever you ask in my name, so that the Father may be glorified in the Son.14 You may ask me for anything in my name, and I will do it.* John 14:12-14

Jesus left us a comforter ,a guide The Holy Spirt. Therefore, we are never alone. Even tough Christ felt forsaken , God was right there in the midst of the pain. Jesus now sits at the right hand of the father making intercession for us. May the peace of God rest, reign and rule in your heart and minds forever. In Jesus name. Amen

A Letter to Caregivers from God

For I know the plans I have for you", "declares the Lord, "plans to prosper you and not to harm you, plans to give you hope and a future.
Jeremiah 29:11

Dear Caregivers,

I know the sacrifices you make on a daily. I know the tears you shed and the pain that you feel inside. The many sacrifices you make that no one sees or acknowledges. They know the glory but they don't know the story.

I see the many nights you spend tossing and turning and trying to figure out what to do and what resources are available to you. Many of you have loss income, stability without reward. I feel your sadness growing heavy as the days, month, years pass by. Every night thoughts of fear, anger, inadequacy runs through your mind. The devil uses your thoughts as playing field to discourage you. But, know I have not given you the spirit fear but, of power, love and a sound mind.

The feelings of self-guilt, not being enough or making a mistake and not having the exact formula for your loved. I know it can be daunting many don't see what you see on a daily basis. They don't know the multitude or magnitude of your gift and contribution to your loved one that will ultimately save their life.

But, I am God I see you, I know you and I hear you. Please know that all your sacrifice and all your labor towards your loved 1 is not in vain. I will reward those who give to the poor who sacrifice and honor the elders. My promise to you is your house will never go empty, your cupboards will never be barren. Financial prosperity will find you won't have to go looking for finances, blessing will come to you. The blessing is in the sacrifice and the detail of the love and support you give your loved one.

I inhabit the praises of my people, I am with you no matter what it looks like, no matter what you sacrifice you have made, I am with you. I see the care you give I know the pain that most will never see and I know the sacrifice.

You shall be rewarded ,you shall be blessed beyond measure. Remember what you have done unto the lest of them you have done unto me. My blessings come to those who give unselfishly to the people around them,

Caregivers you are special and dear to my heart, if no one tells you please know you are the ones that makes that make the world go around, Its your love and sacrifice that sustains the human race. Be assured that if you don't faint in well doing you shall reap a harvest. Every mans harvest is different, so do not covet what your brother or sister has. Don't' be anxious for nothing but in everything by prayer and supplication, with thanksgiving, let your request be made known to God; and the peace of God which passes all understanding ,will guard your hearts and minds through Christ Jesus. Love Always God

WRITTEN BY:

Angelina Y. George
AUTHOR, CAREGIVER AND ENTREPRENEUR

Born and raised in the vibrant state of California, Angelina George has always had a deep connection to faith, family, and community. As a preacher's kid, Angelina grew up immersed in the teachings and values of the church, which laid the foundation for a life dedicated to service and ministry.

Now residing on the East Coast, Angelina continues to carry the legacy of faith through active involvement in multiple church ministries. Whether leading worship, organizing community outreach, or providing pastoral care, Angelina George's dedication to serving others is evident in every aspect of their life.

In addition to ministry, Ms. George embraces the profound role of caregiver. As a full-time caregiver for their mother, who is battling Alzheimer's, Ms. George navigates the challenges and rewards of this journey with grace and resilience. This personal experience has deepened Ms. George's compassion and understanding for caregivers, inspiring and supporting other caregiver's similar situations. Also, MS. George has a course on Udemny.com entitled Overnight Caregiver to help families del with the challenge of caregiving and avoid mistakes in the caregiving process. As Instructor Ms. George was inspired to write the book Overnight Caregiver that can be purchased on Amazon and www.blackgirlpublishing.com this summer.

Balancing caregiving and ministry, Ms. George also channels her creativity and entrepreneurial spirit into her business, Black Girl Publishing.com. Through this platform, Ms. George empowers and amplifies the voices of underrepresented writers, providing them with the tools and opportunities to share their stories with the world.

As a prolific author, Ms. Angelina George has penned eleven books, each reflecting a unique blend of personal insight, spiritual guidance, and storytelling prowess. These works have touched the lives of many, offering inspiration, encouragement, and a sense of connection to readers across the globe. Through all their endeavors, Ms. George exemplifies a life of purpose, driven by faith, love, and an unwavering commitment to making a positive impact in the world.

God Is the Bread of Life

"JESUS SAID TO THEM, 'I AM THE BREAD OF LIFE; WHOEVER COMES TO ME SHALL NOT HUNGER, AND WHOEVER BELIEVES IN ME SHALL NEVER THIRST.'"
(JOHN 6:35)

Prayer For Help to Forgive and Release Hurt

"Bear with each other and forgive one another if any of you has a grievance against someone. Forgive as the Lord forgave you."
(Colossians 3:13)

Lord, my heart feels heavy with pain, and I struggle to overcome the hurt others have caused me. But I come to You, the One who forgave me completely, asking for Your grace to do the same.

Help me release the bitterness and anger that bind me, for I know they only steal my peace. Fill my heart with Your healing love and remind me that forgiveness is not only a gift to others but a pathway to my freedom.

Restore the joy that hurt has taken from me and renew my strength as I lean on Your unending grace.

Amen.

Prayer For Strength to Let Go of Resentment

"Get rid of all bitterness, rage, and anger, along with every form of malice. Be kind and compassionate to one another, forgiving each other, just as in Christ God forgave you."
(Ephesians 4:31-32)

Father, I admit that resentment has taken root in my heart. It's hard to let go of the anger I feel, but I know holding on only separates me from Your peace. Give me the courage and strength to release these feelings to You.

Wash over me with Your love, replacing bitterness with compassion and kindness. Renew my mind so I can see others with the grace You have shown me. Restore my spirit, Lord, and guide me to walk in love and forgiveness as You intended.

Amen.

Prayer For Healing and Renewed Perspective

"But if you do not forgive others their sins, your Father will not forgive your sins."
(Matthew 6:15)

Heavenly Father, I come to You, knowing that forgiveness is not always easy. The wounds in my heart feel raw, and the pain lingers, but I desire to follow Your will.

Heal the broken places within me and renew my perspective. Teach me to see forgiveness not as a weakness, but as a strength—a way to experience the healing and freedom You promise. Strengthen my heart to forgive fully, even when it's hard, and remind me that as I release the pain to You, I am set free.

Amen.

Prayer For Freedom Through Forgiveness

"Come to me, all you who are weary and burdened, and I will give you rest."
(Matthew 11:28)

Lord Jesus, I feel so weary carrying the weight of hurt and unforgiveness. It has burdened my heart and clouded my mind. Today, I choose to lay it all at Your feet.

Take this pain, Lord, and exchange it for Your rest and peace. Restore my soul with Your healing love and renew my thoughts with Your truth. Teach me to forgive fully and completely, as You have forgiven me, and lead me into the freedom that only You can give.

Amen.

Prayer For a Renewed Heart and Mind

"Create in me a pure heart, O God, and renew a steadfast spirit within me."
(Psalm 51:10)

Merciful God, I bring my broken heart before You, longing for Your cleansing touch. Remove every trace of unforgiveness and bitterness that has taken hold.

Create in me a heart that seeks peace, a heart that reflects Your love. Renew my mind, Lord, transforming my thoughts from pain to grace, from anger to love. Strengthen my spirit to leave the hurt behind and embrace the wholeness and freedom You offer. Thank You for Your power to make all things new.

Amen.

WRITTEN BY:

Charlotte Ellis Colbert

GIFTED SONGSTRESS, CERTIFIED LIFE COACH, MOTIVATIONAL SPEAKER, ACCOMPLISHED AUTHOR, AND RECORDING ARTIST

Charlotte Ellis-Colbert carries forward a legacy of faith, service, and dedication. She is the proud daughter of Evangelist Gladys Simmons-Ellis and Earnest Ellis Jr. of Gainesville, FL, and is a devoted mother to three children, Dwan Colbert Jr., Taylor Colbert, and Jaden

Colbert. She is a gifted songstress, certified life coach, motivational speaker, accomplished author, and recording artist. Her literary contributions are co-authoring "Can Anything Good Come from the USA" and "Manifestation Now: Believe, Trust, and Walk Out Your Destiny."

She graduated from Buchholz High School and was blessed to further her education at Tuskegee University where she received her bachelor's degree in education. She holds a master's degree in executive leadership and is pursuing a doctorate, demonstrating her commitment to lifelong learning and excellence. She is also a member of Delta Sigma Theta Incorporated. Charlotte has a heart for service and is deeply committed to helping those in need, while consistently seeking God for wisdom and guidance in her life. Graced as a celebrated psalmist, she has performed alongside gospel greats such as Beverly Crawford, Marvin Sapp, Myron Butler, Dorinda Clarke, and many others. In addition to rendering her singing gift in live studio recordings, such as the "Diary of a Psalmist" (Marvin Sapp) and "Live from The Potter's House." (Bishop T.D. Jakes), she has graced the stage at iconic venues like The Potter's House in Dallas, TX, and has recorded with esteemed producers, including Kevin Bond, Bishop T.D. Jakes, and Stephen Lawrence.

Charlotte serves in the Divine Healing Ministry, founded by her mom, Evangelist Gladys Simmons-Ellis, which continuously brings hope and inspiration to countless lives. She is blessed to serve as an instrumental part of the annual Divine Healing Ministry Back to Basics Benefit Concert sponsored by Divine Healing Ministry. Each year this event offers hope and resources to struggling families while sharing the message of Jesus Christ. The dynamic mother-daughter duo is also working on a gospel recording that promises to uplift and inspire audiences everywhere. Charlotte Ellis Colbert is an extraordinary woman of faith and is humbled at the many giftings God has entrusted her with.

God Is the Vine

"I AM THE VINE; YOU ARE THE BRANCHES.
WHOEVER ABIDES IN ME AND I IN HIM, HE IT
IS THAT BEARS MUCH FRUIT, FOR APART
FROM ME YOU CAN DO NOTHING."
(JOHN 15:5)

Prayer For Physical Healing and Spiritual Renewal

"He heals the brokenhearted and binds up their wounds."
(Psalm 147:3)

Heavenly Father, I come before You, seeking Your healing touch upon my body. You are the Creator of all things and know every cell of my being. Please restore what is broken, ease my pain, and bring my body back to health.

As You heal my physical body, Lord, renew my spirit and strengthen my faith. Help me to trust Your perfect plan and to find peace in Your presence. Let my healing be a testimony of Your love and power.

Amen.

Prayer For Wholeness in Body, Mind, and Spirit

"Do not be anxious about anything, but in every situation, by prayer and petition, with thanksgiving, present your requests to God."
(Philippians 4:6)

Gracious God, I present my whole self—body, mind, and spirit—before You. My body feels weak, and my mind is burdened, but I know You are the source of all healing.

Restore my physical health and renew my thoughts to focus on Your truth. Strengthen my spirit so that I may find joy and peace in You, even during this trial. Thank You for being my refuge and my Healer.

Amen.

Prayer For Healing and Strength

"But those who hope in the Lord will renew their strength. They will soar on wings like eagles." (Isaiah 40:31)

Lord, I place my hope in You, my Healer and Sustainer. My body is tired, and my spirit feels heavy, but I trust in Your promise to renew my strength. Pour out Your healing power over my physical body and uplift my spirit.

Refresh my mind with thoughts of hope and truth and help me rise above this challenge. I know that with You, I can overcome all things.

Amen.

Prayer For Restoration and Peace

"The Lord gives strength to his people; the Lord blesses his people with peace."
(Psalm 29:11)

Father, I seek Your healing and peace over my body and mind. Touch every area of my physical being that needs restoration. Calm the storm of anxiety and worry within me and renew my spirit with Your peace that transcends understanding.

Help me to trust in Your care and to rest in Your love. May Your strength carry me through this time, and may Your healing bring wholeness to every part of me.

Amen.

Prayer For Complete Renewal

"Create in me a pure heart, O God, and renew a steadfast spirit within me."
(Psalm 51:10)

Lord, I ask for complete renewal—heal my body of sickness, cleanse my mind of fear, and restore my spirit with Your joy. Create in me a heart that is steadfast and focused on You.

Let Your healing power flow through every part of me, bringing vitality to my body and clarity to my thoughts. Strengthen my faith and fill me with Your peace. Thank You, Lord, for Your boundless mercy and grace.

Amen.

WRITTEN BY:

Evangelist Gladys Simmons-Ellis
EVANGELIST

Evangelist Gladys Simmons-Ellis is a devoted servant of God and a cherished daughter of the Church of God by Faith (COGBF). She has been a lifelong member of Jerusalem COGBF in Monteocha, Florida, where she has faithfully served for decades.

In 1999, she received her ministerial and evangelist license, solidifying hercommitment to spreading the gospel.

Her journey in ministry began early, as she started singing at the age of eight alongside her sisters in their group, the Simmons Sisters. Standing on a stool so she could be seen, young Gladys captivated audiences with her powerful voice. Known for their spirited praise and worship, the Simmons Sisters traveled extensively, proclaiming the gospel in song and even recording several of their pieces.

At 75 years old, Evangelist Ellis remains a vibrant force for the kingdom of God. She is a wife (Earnest Ellis Jr.), mother (Napoleon Ellis and Charlotte Ellis Colbert), and grandmother/great-grandmother. She is co-author of "Can Anything Good Come from the USA." She touches lives through her teaching, singing, and unwavering praise. She is a graduate of A.L. Mebane High School and Santa Fe Community College. Evangelist Ellis retired as a surgical tech specialist at Shands Teaching Hospital, where her compassionate spirit and bold faith allowed her to witness to doctors and pray with patients, leaving an enduring legacy of love and encouragement. In 2000, Evangelist Ellis founded Divine Healing Ministry, an outreach dedicated to providing clothing, food, and monetary assistance for housing and additional needs. With her daughter, Charlotte Ellis-Colbert, she sponsors the annual Divine Healing Ministry Back to Basics Benefit Concert, offering hope and resources to struggling families while sharing the message of Jesus Christ.

Evangelist Ellis is also a living testimony of God's healing power. Diagnosed with Myasthenia Gravis, a neuromuscular disorder, in 2021, she experienced both divine healing and medical intervention, enabling her to continue sharing her powerful story of faith and God's miraculous grace. Her unwavering dedication to her family, community, and ministry makes her a true inspiration and a beacon of light in North Central Florida.

God Is Our Provider

"THE LORD IS MY SHEPHERD; I SHALL NOT WANT."
(PSALM 23:1)

Created in His Image

So God created human beings in his own image. In the image of God he created them; male and female he created them.
Genesis 1:27 (NLT)

Father in the name of JESUS:
Thank You for creating me in Your image, with care, intention, and love. As I reflect on the beauty of Your creation, I honor each part of my body as a reflection of Your divine design.

Lord, I thank You for my mind, shaped to think with wisdom, creativity, and purpose. Let my thoughts align with Your truth and bring glory to Your name. I thank You for my eyes, which You have crafted to see the wonders of this world and to recognize Your hand in all things. Help me to look at others with compassion and love, just as You see me.

I praise You for my mouth, given to speak life, declare truth, and share the gospel. Guard my words, Lord, that they may reflect Your grace. Thank You for my hands, designed to create, build, and serve others as an extension of Your love. May they always do Your work.

Father, I thank You for my feet, which carry me to places You've called me to go. Guide my steps, so I walk in Your will.

Lord, I am fearfully and wonderfully made, created in Your image. May my whole being reflect Your glory. Amen.

Blessing the Mind, Body, and Soul Through God's Perfect Will

Father in the name of JESUS, I come before You today with a humble heart and an open mind, seeking to align my thoughts with Yours.

Your Word declares, "As a man thinketh in his heart, so is he" (Proverbs 23:7). I recognize that my thoughts shape my identity, my actions, and my future. Lord, renew my mind and cleanse it of any thoughts that are not rooted in Your truth, love, and purpose. Let my mind reflect the perfection of Your will, bringing alignment to my entire being.

Bless my mind, Lord, that it may meditate on what is pure, noble, and worthy of praise. Bless my eyes, that I may see the vision You have for me. Bless my ears, that I may hear Your voice and reject the lies of the enemy. Bless my mouth, that I may speak words of life and faith. Bless my heart, that it may overflow with Your wisdom, joy, and peace. Bless my hands and feet, that they may serve and walk according to Your will.

Father, I align myself with the truth that whole body blessings flow from the mind You renew. As my thoughts transform, my body, actions, and spirit are brought into divine harmony. I declare that my entire being is consecrated to You—mind, body, and soul. Let Your thoughts become my thoughts, Your blessings flow through every part of me, and Your will guide every step.

In Jesus' name, Amen.

Hands Lifted in Worship and Service

Lord, I lift my hands to You as an act of worship, surrender, and thanksgiving. These hands You have given me are a blessing, tools to serve You and others.

When I lift them, I declare that I honor You above all else. Lifting my hands reminds me of Your sovereignty and my dependence on Your strength.

Lord, as my hands reach toward heaven, I feel the connection to Your presence. It's a reminder that I am never alone—that Your power, grace, and mercy flow freely into my life. Thank You for the blessing of these hands, capable of creating, helping, and holding.

Bless my hands, Lord, as I use them to glorify You. Let them build, heal, and uplift, never destroy or harm. When I lift them in worship, may it be a testimony of my love and devotion to You. Thank You for the privilege of using my whole body, especially my hands, to declare Your greatness.

In Jesus' name, Amen.

Blessing the Gift of Vision

Father in the name of JESUS, I thank You for the gift of vision. My eyes, which You so wonderfully created, are not just physical tools to see the world but spiritual instruments to perceive Your purpose for my life. Lord, I ask You to bless my eyes that they may always see clearly—not only the beauty of Your creation but also the opportunities to serve and love others.

Help me to see through the lens of faith and not fear. Let my eyes focus on the good and the godly, not the distractions or distortions of this world. Give me the clarity to discern Your will and the wisdom to see beyond what is temporary and into what is eternal.

May my eyes be a blessing to others as I look upon them with compassion, kindness, and understanding. Let them reflect Your light and truth. Thank You for the vision to dream, plan, and pursue the life You've called me to live. In Jesus' name, Amen.

A Heart Aligned with God's Will

Father, I thank You for my heart, the center of my emotions, thoughts, and love. It is a precious gift, created by You to carry Your love and reflect it to the world. I ask You to bless my heart that it may remain pure, tender, and open to Your guidance.

Lord, let my heart beat in rhythm with Your will, full of love for You and others. Protect it from bitterness, anger, or fear, and instead, fill it with Your joy, peace, and understanding. Let my heart be a place where Your Spirit dwells, guiding my decisions and shaping my actions.

Help me to guard my heart, knowing that everything I do flows from it. May it always be a vessel of faith and courage, responding to the challenges of life with trust in Your promises. Thank You for this heart, which connects my whole body to Your purpose. I

n Jesus' name, Amen.

WRITTEN BY:

Donna Izzard

BEST-SELLING AMAZON AUTHOR, INTERNATIONAL SPEAKER, WOMEN EMPOWERMENT LEADER AND ENTREPRENEUR

Donna Izzard has a passionate vision that she tirelessly puts to use in the service of others. As an international speaker, Donna speaks candidly about her life experience and shares her truth and hard-earned wisdom with others to uplift and inspire as many as she can.

As an entrepreneur and best-selling author, she has launched and managed a successful business while working as Deputy Chief of Operations at an AmLaw100 law firm. It is her 30+ years spent in Corporate America that has honed her God-given gift for innovation and ability to bring out the inner, often hidden, phenomenal in people.

Donna turned what began as an empowerment workshop in her childhood community of Harlem into the Unstoppable Black Woman (UBW) sisterhood, a thriving movement for Black women. Through workshops and trainings for UBW, Donna inspires Black women to embrace an unstoppable mindset. Donna regularly hosts free local workshops on self-esteem, confidence and entrepreneurship. She has also published life-changing books, which motivate Black women and children to always keep moving forward.

For several years, Donna was the business manager for the former White House Ambassador of Religious Freedom Reverend Dr. Suzan D. Johnson Cook.
Donna has been honored with the Women In Ministry Worldwide Award given by Reverend Al Sharpton's National Action Networks Women's Auxiliary New York City Chapter for the critical work she has done in the community and ministry.

Donna was identified as one of the top coaches to watch by the Huffington Post and was recognized as one of 30 Black Global Leaders by Impact Magazine, a lifestyle publication whose mission is to empower, encourage and educate readers through the power of images and words. Donna was most recently selected as a Notable Black Leader by Crain's New York Business, an honor that identifies talented and accomplished Black individuals whose professional and communal achievements enhance New York City and the lives of its inhabitants.

God Is Our Banner

THE LORD IS MY BANNER."
(EXODUS 17:15)

Prayer of Steadfastness

Father in the name of Jesus, I come before your throne, thanking you for your grace and tender mercies. I am grateful for you being my blessed assurance. A God that is Faithful to his word. You promised to never leave me, nor forsake me (Hebrews 13:5) and that you will be a present help in the time of trouble.

Therefore, I decree and declare that I will be steadfast in my faith. I will not be moved by what my eyes see, neither will I agree with fear and doubt. I walk by faith and not by sight.

The just shall live by faith. As a child of God, I will be steadfast, in the things of God, unmovable, always abounding in the works of the Lord. Knowing that my labor, my faith, my salvation is not in vain.

I thank you Father for keeping my heart and mind in perfect peace. I bless and glorify your holy name. In Jesus Name I pray and believe, Amen.

WRITTEN BY:

Apostle Chiquita Clark

SPEAKER AND PASTOR

Apostle Chiquita is more than just a speaker or pastor. She has been declared as a modern day "Deborah". She is one who will help aid the people of God with wisdom and righteousness. She is the founder of Restoration Worship Center in Lavonia, Georgia, where she serves alongside her husband, Bishop Bruce Clark.

With more than twenty plus years serving in ministry, Apostle Chiquita's speaking engagements, leadership tips, and life experiences have helped many people navigate through some of life's most challenging dilemmas. Standing firm on the words of God and maintaining a strong prayer life is the essence of Apostle Chiquita triumphing over her own setbacks and disappointments in life; In addition to overcoming fear of failure and fear of success.

On August 3, 2018, while attending a conference in Raleigh, North Carolina, Apostle Chiquita launched her ministry, "Emerging Beyond". This ministry is purposed to mentoring and equipping individuals, as well as other ministries and businesses of one's ability to aid and assist in advancing the kingdom with his or her gifts.

No longer will we remain silent. God have given us power to Unleash our voice.

Chiquita obtained her Business Administration Associates Degree from Forest College in Anderson, SC. In 2003, Chiquita became a licensed Realtor in the state of Georgia. She is a professional certified Life Coach by the International Coach Federation and a certified Christian Mentor obtained through P4 Coaching Institution. She and her husband reside less than two hours from Atlanta, Georgia in the beautiful Northeast Georgia area. Her greatest asset is being a Child of God, wife, mother and Gigi to her beautiful grandchildren.

- Chiquita Clark
- @iamchiquitaclark

A Prayer of Comfort

Dear God, I pray for those of us who are in need a special blessing from You. So many of Your children are facing difficult times today. I pray that we feel the embrace of Your love surrounding us.

I pray that the Holy Spirit comforts us and leads us to a place of peace. Help your children to find complete rest in You. Let us know that we are never alone, that Your presence is always there. Your Word promises that there are many benefits available to us. You are our healer, our redeemer. You satisfy our desires with good things.

I pray that we discover that Your wisdom is available to us. Let us not grow weary. I pray that we receive the ability to allow Your gifts to flow freely through us. I pray that once we are healed and made whole, that we will be mindful to give You all the glory, honor and praise.

In Jesus name, I pray. Amen

WRITTEN BY:

La Verne Marie Byrd
AUTHOR AND SPEAKER

LaVerne Marie Byrd is a native Washingtonian. Her most recent publication, Heal My Pain, A Journal for Grieving Mothers, was written to help other moms during their grief journey. LaVerne has spoken on the topic of grief on many occasions.

She believes that there needs to be more conversations about grief and the healing journey. She was interviewed by Dr. Ted Rynearson. a clinical psychiatrist, as well as a national and international clinical teacher.

LaVerne shared how the trauma of losing a child affected her and how she was able to use journaling and professional counseling to process her grief.

LaVerne has also contributed essays in several editions of the Community Book Project, Celebrating 365 Days of Gratitude.

She believes in the power of gratitude, and it is always her desire to encourage and uplift others.

 thejourneyofgrief.com

Today is Your Receiving Day!

We have been redeemed from the kingdom of darkness, which means we have been redeemed from poverty, lack, and debt. But sometimes we get so caught up in the stressors of life that we forget we have been redeemed. God longs to lavish us with His blessings each day. Yet, we must learn how to receive His overwhelming goodness.

Receiving is an inside job. We receive on the inside before we receive on the outside. When you choose to believe God's promises, you cast away worry. First you believe. Then you receive.

Your faith is the power button that turns on manifestation. It puts you in position to receive. Your only job is to believe and receive. The manifestation is not your job. God will do the manifesting. You just keep believing and receiving by faith by declaring His promises over your life. Thank you, God, today is my receiving day!

Your miracle is waiting for you. It's waiting for your faith to show up. Faith expects. A spirit of expectancy says, "Today is my receiving day!"

WRITTEN BY:

Patti Fagan

CHRISTIAN AUTHOR, BLOGGER & COACH

Patti Fagan is a sought-after speaker, trauma-informed Christian life coach, Ramsey Solutions Master Financial Coach, Certified Holistic Health Coach, author of 12+ nonfiction books, and a former retirement planner.

She is passionate about empowering Christians to thrive in every area of their lives, especially in their finances.

Patti is called to help believers heal their relationship with money and conquer financial lack, so they can prosper in the kingdom of God.

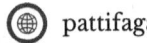 pattifagan.com

Prayer Of Inspiration

Dear Lord,

As I bow before You in humility, I seek the wellspring of inspiration that flows from Your boundless love and wisdom. I recognize that You are the Creator of all that is beautiful, the Source of every idea, and the spark of creativity that ignites the hearts of those who seek Your truth. I come to You today, longing for Your guidance to fill my spirit and enlighten my mind.

Lord, inspire me to see the world through Your eyes—to recognize the beauty in the mundane and the potential in every challenge I face. Help me to cultivate a heart that is open to new ideas, and grant me the courage to explore uncharted territories. May Your Spirit stir within me, igniting a passion for discovery and a thirst for knowledge that cannot be quenched.

In times of uncertainty, when doubt clouds my vision, I ask that You grant me clarity. Help me to discern the path that aligns with Your divine purpose for my life. May I find comfort in Your promises and strength in Your presence as I navigate the complexities of my journey. Fill me with the assurance that I am guided by Your hand, even when the way seems unclear.

Lord, inspire me to be a beacon of hope and positivity to those around me. Let my words and actions reflect Your love and grace, encouraging others to seek their own paths of inspiration. Teach me to listen deeply to the hearts of others, offering support and understanding, and to celebrate their victories as if they were my own.

As I strive to fulfill the unique calling You have placed upon my life, grant me the discipline to pursue my passions with dedication. Help me to overcome the barriers of fear and self-doubt that may hinder my progress. Let Your Spirit embolden me to take risks, to step outside my comfort zone, and to embrace the unknown, knowing that I am never alone on this journey.

In moments of despair or creative block, remind me of Your faithfulness and the myriad ways You inspire those who seek You. Let me draw from the well of Your wisdom and reflect on the countless stories of those who have overcome obstacles through faith and determination. May their journeys ignite a flame within me, urging me to persevere in my own pursuit of inspiration.

Lord, may I also be a source of inspiration to others. Help me to share my gifts freely, encouraging those around me to embrace their own uniqueness. Let me uplift and empower, shining a light in the lives of those who may feel lost or discouraged. Teach me the value of collaboration, reminding me that we are stronger together, united in our shared purpose to make the world a better place.

Thank You, Lord, for the creativity that flows through each of us and for the inspiration that comes from our connection to You. I am grateful for the moments of insight and clarity that You provide, and I pray that I may remain ever receptive to Your guiding hand. As I seek to live a life of purpose, may Your inspiration be my constant companion.

In Your holy name, I pray. Amen.

WRITTEN BY:

Prophetess Demeka Vines

CEO GAFF & ASSOCIATES AND FOUNDER OF GODLY
AFFIRMATIONS ONLINE PRAYER MINISTRY

Prophetess Demeka Vines, a devoted minister, author, registered nurse, and mother, hails from Greenville, NC. She is the visionary founder of Godly Affirmations, INC, an online intercessory ministry on Facebook dedicated to fostering encouragement, spiritual growth, and reconciliation with Christ Jesus within its community.

Currently, Demeka is advancing her education as a graduate student in the Family Nurse Practitioner program, specializing in Psychiatric Mental Health, with the goal of becoming a licensed therapist.

Through her unwavering commitment to service and her faith, she aims to be a transformative force in the lives of others, inspiring them to deepen their spiritual journeys and pursue healing.

(f) Demeka Vines

(🌐) www.authordemekavines.com

Relentless Faith

Gracious and loving Father,

Thank You for Your abundant grace that never runs dry. Thank You for blessing me beyond measure, for providing all I need in every moment. You are so faithful, and I praise You for being my unshakable source of strength and hope.

Lord, I come before You with a humble heart, aware of the times I have fallen short—when I've doubted Your sufficiency or allowed fear to silence my faith. Forgive me for the ways I've held back, for the times I've chosen comfort over obedience. Wash me clean and set my heart right before You.

You are able, God. You are powerful, and nothing is impossible for You. Help me to trust that fully. Fill me with courage to walk in Your plans, even when they stretch me or feel uncertain. I want to abound in every good work. You've prepared for me, to be Your vessel of love and grace to the world around me.

Today, I say "yes" to You, Lord. Yes to Your power at work in me. Yes to the purpose You've called me to. Lead me, guide me, and strengthen me to live out this calling with boldness and joy. I surrender it all to You, trusting You will supply all I need.

In Jesus' Name I pray, Amen.

WRITTEN BY:

Benecia Ponder
BOOK WRITING & PUBLISHING COACH

Benecia Ponder is a Book Writing & Publishing Coach to Inspirational Authors—purpose-driven entrepreneurs who share their life experiences and expertise through powerful stories that inspire and impact lives.

Find out more at InspirationalAuthors.com.

- (f) @beneciaponder
- (ig) @beneciaponder
- (in) www.linkedin.com/in/beneciaponder
- (X) BeneciaPonder
- @beneciaponder
- (▶) @inspirationalauthors93

God Is Our Refuge in the Storm

"YOU HAVE BEEN A REFUGE FOR THE POOR, A REFUGE FOR THE NEEDY IN THEIR DISTRESS, A SHELTER FROM THE STORM AND A SHADE FROM THE HEAT."
(ISAIAH 25:4)

Trusting in God's Healing Process

Gracious Father,

You are the Creator of our bodies, minds, and spirits, and today we trust You as the ultimate healer. Lord, teach us to be patient in the process of restoration, knowing that Your timing is perfect and Your ways are higher than ours.

When our healing feels delayed or uncertain, remind us of Your promises. Help us to trust that You are working in every moment, weaving together a testimony of wholeness and grace. Let us find peace in knowing that You hold every part of us in Your loving hands.

Father, as we walk this journey of healing, strengthen our faith and renew our hope. Let Your Spirit fill us with patience and calm, guiding our hearts to rest in Your care. May we encourage others who are waiting for their own breakthroughs, sharing the hope that comes from Your love.

Thank You, Lord, for being our healer and sustainer. Let our trust in Your process be a reflection of the faith we have in Your boundless power and compassion.

In Jesus' name, Amen.

Grateful for the Gift of Health

Heavenly Father,

You have fearfully and wonderfully made us, and today we pause to thank You for the gift of health. Lord, teach us to value and steward the bodies You have entrusted to us. Let gratitude overflow as we reflect on the ways You sustain and restore us each day.

When we face challenges in our health, remind us of the victories You have already won for us. Let Your Spirit cultivate contentment within us, allowing us to see Your hand in every aspect of our healing journey. May our gratitude strengthen our spirits and bring glory to Your name.

Father, guide us to use the health we have to serve others and further Your kingdom. Let our lives be a testimony to the joy that comes from walking in alignment with Your will. May we inspire those around us to honor the blessings of life and health.

Thank You for being our sustainer and healer, Lord. Let our hearts always reflect gratitude for Your endless mercy and provision.

In Jesus' name, Amen.

Strengthening the Whole Body in God's Power

Mighty Healer,

You are the source of our strength and vitality, and today we pray for the restoration of our whole bodies. Lord, equip us with the energy and resilience needed to fulfill the purpose You have set before us.

When our bodies feel weak or our spirits falter, remind us that Your strength is made perfect in our weakness. Teach us to rely on Your Spirit for renewal, trusting in Your power to bring us into complete healing and wholeness.

Father, as we experience Your strength, help us to encourage others who feel weary. Let us share the hope of restoration found in You, bringing comfort and inspiration to those who are struggling. May our lives reflect the vitality that comes from walking in step with Your Spirit.

Thank You, Lord, for being our constant sustainer. Let us honor You by caring for our whole selves—body, mind, and spirit—and using our strength to glorify You.

In Jesus' name, Amen.

Love that Heals Every Part

Faithful Lord,

You have knit us together with care, and today we pray for Your healing love to flow through every part of our being. Lord, touch our bodies, minds, and spirits, bringing renewal and wholeness as only You can.

When we feel the weight of sickness or weariness, remind us of Your unending compassion. Teach us to rest in Your presence, allowing Your love to restore what is broken and strengthen what feels weak. Let Your Spirit bring peace and hope, guiding us toward complete healing.

Father, help us to extend this love to others, becoming instruments of encouragement and healing in their lives. Let our testimonies of renewal point them to the power and beauty of Your love. May our lives reflect the wholeness that comes from being fully known and cared for by You.

Thank You for being the God who heals, Lord. Let our hearts and bodies always rest in the abundance of Your love.

In Jesus' name, Amen.

Prayer for Patience: Trusting in God's Timing

Sovereign Lord,

You work all things for our good, and today we pray for patience. Lord, teach us to trust in Your perfect timing, knowing that Your plans are far greater than our own.

When we feel restless or frustrated, remind us that You are always at work, even when we cannot see it. Let Your Spirit guide our hearts, filling us with peace and understanding. May we find joy in the process of waiting, trusting that You are preparing us for something greater.

Father, as we learn patience, help us to extend grace to others. Let our lives reflect the calm assurance that comes from trusting in Your timing, inspiring those around us to wait on You.

Thank You for being the God who is always on time, Lord. Let our patience glorify You and strengthen our faith.

In Jesus' name, Amen.

WRITTEN BY:

Dr. Renee Sunday, MD

THE KINGDOM BUILDER - ANESTHESIOLOGIST, MEDIA MOGUL, ORDAINED MINISTER & PODCASTER

Dr. Renee Sunday, an award-winning, board-certified Anesthesiologist, carries a passion to act as a catalyst and inspire individuals to move towards their destined path. She is an esteemed founder of DRS Global and Renee Sunday Enterprises, including Sunday Publishing Company, showcasing her entrepreneurial prowess.

Not just limited to the medical field, Dr. Sunday has also successfully planted her roots in the media industry. She is a prominent podcaster, television personality, and the esteemed host of the Good Deeds TV Show and Magazine. Through her podcast show, she channels her wisdom and uplifts her audience.

Her life took a spiritual turn growing up in a Christian family, where her interest in spirituality and philanthropy led her to become a minister. Realizing people's struggles in their spiritual journeys, she felt the need to guide them.

Dr. Sunday thrives on being a tool in God's Plan, extending love, compassion, and a high standard of care to others. Her mission is to empower people to bring their message to the world, believing that everyone has a purpose, a calling, and a unique reason to be alive. She acknowledges that people often question their existence and purpose in life and assures them that one's purpose can span across multiple areas reflecting their diverse interests.

- (f) Dr.reneesundaythekingdombuilder
- (ig) @reneesundaymd
- (🌐) reneesunday.com

God Is Our Deliverer

"I SOUGHT THE LORD, AND HE ANSWERED ME
AND DELIVERED ME FROM ALL MY FEARS."
(PSALM 34:4)

Stay Connected

WHOLE BODY BLESSINGS: DIVINE HEALING PRAYER COLLECTION

Stay Connected

Join us on YouTube for prayers, reflections, and inspiring content to deepen your Christian journey.

Subscribe to stay encouraged and uplifted!

www.ingramcontent.com/pod-product-compliance
Lightning Source LLC
Chambersburg PA
CBHW070639160426
43194CB00009B/1502